73

My, My, My, My, My
Tara Hardy

ೞ

Write Bloody Publishing
America's Independent Press

Los Angeles, CA
WRITEBLOODY.COM

Hardy, Tara.
1ˢᵗ edition.

Edited by Sarah Brickman
Proofread by Keaton Maddox
Cover Design by Zoe Norvell
Interior Layout by Kayla Shelley

Type set in Bergamo from www.theleagueofmoveabletype.com

ISBN 978-1938912-64-1

Write Bloody Publishing
Los Angeles, CA

Support Independent Presses
writebloody.com

To contact the author, send an email to writebloody@gmail.com

MADE IN THE USA

Μγ, Μγ, Μγ, Μγ, Μγ

For Tamara Lewis

Rhegnunai

Haima

Tortile

Chimera

Gignoskein

Hemostasis

Rhegnunai
(To burst forth.)

Security is mostly a superstition.
—Hellen Keller

Wrinkle

There is a place called Land of the Sick
we ferret away, tuck under
the map, ignore bulges under New
Jersey and Detroit where industrial stacks
send droves of us to beg under broken
smiles of free-care hospitals. But when it comes
to it, not even the rich can outwit the white-
breathed furnace that will claim all

of us. This is why we hide
the evidence. Like a mother trying
to hide her cigarettes. If we
had the sick walking among us
they might remind us that we are
as frail as the simple failure
of a blood test. That's how it happened
for me—what are these spots
on my legs? And suddenly,
I've stepped through a wrinkle
in the fabric of privilege.

Day Before You Were Yourself

On the day "chemotherapy" becomes a word
relevant to your life you will not
scream. You will close in on yourself
like a spider going rigor
mortis, hard, hollow-limbed,
curl feebly to protect organs.

That night when a spider appears
in your bedroom, you will want to step
toe-ball on it, but instead capture
it in apparatus of Tupperware
and manila folder, shunt

the body through a flap in the screen while feeling
nothing. You will do this, because—
it will be what you do. In the morning, the howl
will begin behind your eyes, your head

will try to shake it off, involuntarily jerk
to the right-left-right.
It may be rush hour,

but suddenly, all around, there will be plenty
of seats on the bus. You won't know
you're bawling until something
wet slaps your shirt. The temporary relief
will allow the world to still
just long enough for an idea

to open: Jump out onto the grass. Go
get the car. Drive to Goodwill. Spend
three hours picking out
the right chemotherapy costume. Purchase
six pink dresses. An extravagance,

even at Goodwill. Pink
is medicine. Pink is Pepto. Pink is peony
beginning to die in your bathroom of whom
no one but last week's daisy is envious.

Being told you're going to have chemotherapy
is like suddenly realizing you're on a zip line.
Maybe you had some cerebral acquaintance
before, but this will be brand new body-

awakening that the contraption
into which you're belted isn't
kidding. No theoretical
here. No religion either, although

you will be joltingly aware
of your soul. New body-knowledge, cold
demanding fact: You have sped
up, the cable above is not only
limited, but fraying. This is not a movie,

but free fall. Always has been. The "safety"
belt has always been optical illusion,

otherwise known as cultural habit
to deny impermanence. On the way
home from Goodwill, while six pink
dresses steam from the passenger seat, anger
will seize the wheel. You will confuse

one foot for the other, accelerator
for brake. The sudden upsurge
on polite street will scatter
crows and scare the mother

with two girls trying to cross
the intersection. She will pull back,
hold the girls' shoulders, scowl,
until she sees
you're weeping. She'll pause, her face
will melt, and then she'll prompt
those chickadees forward, wave.

You'll think of your ex-husband, who left
for a younger woman with a functional
womb, "Bet he's glad I couldn't
have his children now that I'm——"

The sight of the girls' retreating backs
will prompt you to scoop-gesture
your chest out, push its fake air-contents
through windshield—please take
whatever-it-was-I-was-supposed-
to-give-my-never-to-be-daughter
and keep it. Put it on
like a pink dress. One of them
will be wearing green, her hair
will glint as she rounds the corner
out of sight.

Listen, there was a day before
you were yourself. There will be a day
after. This is what is
called eternity. It's the only thing we get to keep
forever.

Charity Hospitals

The rooms of our woolen bodies
slumped over sides
of chairs stink like free chemicals
and hope. Charity hospitals
are simultaneously the kindest
and most rutted of places. I can't forget
our shoes, plastic, bowed, click
of cheap material on overly polished
floors. So many costumes. I played
good girl. Some donned
forlorn. Others had been in that rut
for so long they didn't bother
to adorn, plot. Merely presented themselves
like the hard rinds of medicine
bottles—indifferent to thumbs.

Transparent

Platelets are small, slightly yellow, mostly transparent
discs that float through your blood to keep you

from bleeding out. Not unlike flat pearls. String
enough of them together and you have something

to catch the wind. Maybe an insect wing. Or lens.
Illness makes other people adjust

their eyesight. Illness makes people put you on
like lenses, perch you atop their noses, look

through you to see themselves. When you become
transparent, suddenly, everyone can see

through you. But they're not looking at you—
they're looking at themselves. I used to

watch movies about people becoming disabled,
wonder how much would be enough

of me left to want to stay alive. This is what I call
the arrogance of my formerly non-disabled body.

I thought about my hands, eyes or mind's sharp
acuity. All my life I've been told

I'm smart. My mother said, "It's a good thing
you're smart, because you're not pretty." Smart

was what I had, so I went,
formed identity, made my living with it.

Don't get me wrong, I'd rather be told any
day that my cheekbones look great in these

jeans, but that's only two things: sexism,
and no matter what I already have

smart. When platelets in your blood are attacked
by your own immune system, the risk

is that you'll stop clotting and your brain
will bleed. When my platelets disappear, petechiae

(small red spots) appear on my knees, then belly,
then chest, then cheeks. One time I found a spot

directly under my right eye. When they tell me I'm at risk
for intracranial hemorrhage, I start to wonder what

is enough. I put on lenses, polish off some other people
I use as microscopes to evaluate my own courage. I think,

just let me keep (thing at the moment that scares me most).
But how could I possibly tolerate not having enough smart

to be a poet? On the way home from eight more brain-scare
days in the hospital, trees are so viciously green. It's a beauty

that feels like it could kill me. I want to stop, get out, shout
to people getting off the bus, "Do you see how green, green

are the trees?" But I guess a better question is can we ever
fully comprehend our riches? If I lose my faculties,

if God decides I am to be distilled into a single taste bud,
I want it. Prop me near a window, bring me

a vanilla bean. They're delicious, and pointed enough
to locate a single bud. Watch yourself open

through the lens I become. Then bring me
my lover one last time, let her push her tongue

into my mouth as if to search for pearl,
for that essential thing that makes me,

me. Translucent as my own private moon, that flat disc
in the sky, we've all prayed to at least once. The concave

lens against which we measure our own
shimmer. Stand close, I promise that distilled

into a single bud, I will still be enough
to illuminate the worth of your own viciously glistening life.

Fatigue

Is not tired, not
"I totally get it, because last week
I worked too much."

Imagine someone has had an individual keg party
in every single one of your muscles, now
imagine it is the morning
after. Imagine that someone has taken
each of your muscles out
of your body, even the ones
the size of a baby sunfish, beaten them
with a meat mallet, then put them

back in. Imagine your bones
are made of smoke,
or whispers.

Imagine scarves are what keep
your skeleton together.
Imagine your sleeves are filled
with pudding; try to make

dinner. Imagine your legs are filled
with marbles; try to walk up stairs

in front of neighbors
on a July day
when everyone is coming back
from a cookout. Try not to feel

rage. Imagine your head
is made of a building;
your forehead is your last regret. Try
to hold them up in front of everyone
at the meeting. Wonder if everyone
is thinking, "Why isn't she in bed?"
Or, "Why is it so hard for her
to sit up (this only lasts an hour)?"

Imagine the hands
of body-builders are holding down
your limbs. Four or so hands around
each limb. "Hey, can you swing
by and drop off that document?"
Imagine the document is made
of an entire old-growth forest.

Imagine you are an old-
growth forest and you need
to relocate. Where do you start?
Which part of you do you preserve

first? Imagine your shoes are filled
with tomorrow, but you're trying to wade through
yesterday. Imagine yesterday
is made of sand
and tomorrow is made
of flood. Imagine there is no sun,

just the promise of one. Every day
you get up thinking, "But this
is where they said it would
be, where the sun would herald
a right to live among the living
again. This is where I find
morning, renewal, tomorrow
that isn't made of night."
If everything is made
of night then how do we ever
get to call it a new day?

The Night Before Chemotherapy

The last thing the doctor will say is, "And you're okay with the viral..."

You're supposed to fill in his sentence. "Yes," you answer.

He'll continue, "The very rare, viral..."

You'll hesitate, gird yourself to look what you hope is enthusiastic, "Yes, the potential brain infection."

"It's very rare," he'll say.

You'll nod, sign the document.

On the way home and for the next seven hours you'll keep hearing the word "viral." Viral, viral, viral. Things such as the Internet will suddenly infuriate you. Why do people use the word viral to describe what happens in virtual space when it's axing down literal people in literal space? When it's wedging itself into their crevices, their bone marrow, their DNA. When viruses, latent in the brain, can be triggered by drugs they administer to try to save you.

Administer in the arm. Hook you up to something from which you can't get away. Can't. Get. Away. It is inside you. A tube inside your veins like your father was inside you, seven years old, and you can't get away. Because what comes inside is trying to fix where you are broken from what he did to you. The illness itself was left behind by fear; he pulled out but terror remained. His after-essence haunting like a fog or a smell, a stench waiting to turn into something real, visible. A flag above an underground sewer, above an underground scream.

Even at the cellular level, I've been fighting back for as long as I've had teeth. Tomorrow, they put something inside me that will at long last try to stop the fighting back. The fight-back grew its own teeth and has turned on me. I have become allergic to myself. This is not a metaphor, but literal emergency. At the biological level of flesh and mortar.

The immune system, it is known, is deregulated by trauma. Unsets itself, twists upside down: a monster has risen up inside me. Tomorrow, they put inside my veins a bigger monster than the one I grew to fight him off. I am still fighting. The way out of this is to stop fighting, but I buried that instinct along with my seven-year-old.

"Yes, I'm okay with the brain virus," is the last thing you'll say aloud, alone before the clock strikes midnight.

When you awkwardly meet your doctor in the elevator in the morning, and it eventually lands on the first floor, hold the door open, like a monster would, for the lady to get out.

Hair Loss

The immune system,
       when on alert,
              just goes around
                    getting rid of shit.
Without mercy. Platelets.
             Hair. Kidney tissue.
      It's like having an abusive
    mother always going through
             your stuff and this abusive mother

             lives inside you.

You don't have her phone number.
          She doesn't have an address,
              except yours.

To shoot her, you'd have to shoot
yourself. Instead, you just pray,
please let my feet still be there
when I get home. Please let me not

digest my own heart muscle.
          Please, let her forget I have a frontal
          lobe. There's no dimmer
          switch. Just a mother whose white
          open laser eyes can find all

                                your hiding spots.

Fear of Bleeding

All my poems look like
razor cuts. I want to write them
                        down
                            the sharp
                                end of
                                    the page.

ThrOugh the Walls

Once, I lOOked at a dOg

    and wOndered why

        dOes that LabradOr

           prOduce platelets?

        Once, I lOOked

    at my dOctOr

        and thOught,

           I suppOse his wife

                pOssesses platelets. Once,

        in a bistrO,

    I lOOked at my spOOn

        and wOndered whO,

           in the rOOm,

                wOuld I nOt gOre

           tO siphOn Out

        sOme platelets?

    There was Only One,

my lOver, and she

    had already Offered

        her platelets. Once,

           I swOre I smelled

my next dOOr

neighbOr's ability to clOt

thrOugh the walls.

Salt in the Wind

For Aubrey Bean

You will be standing in the market, sorting through avocados when the band Kansas, "Dust in the Wind," will come pumping through the ceiling. And you'll think, "Jesus, this song is gonna outlive me."

There are a few things that getting really sick illuminates:

One: Dieting is ridiculous. How you look is beside the point. The biggest gift you bring to any room is your heart.

Two: You will ask anyone for money, will get on your knees to beg your enemy for help, because you know that deep down under all that animosity is a deep and abiding love. For why else would she hate you with such loyalty?

Three: Things that used to taste bitter suddenly turn to maple sugar in your mouth. What you wouldn't give for another year to grieve that man you thought you loved more than your own bone marrow.

Four: Suddenly everything will be so beautiful—the halfhearted sunset, rotting leaves. The way a rind hugs a lime. Your own age spots—what you wouldn't do to earn more of them.

Five: Yes, you will drink liquid seaweed. Hell, you'd stand on your head in a mini skirt wearing no underpants in front of your ex's new girlfriend if you thought it would make a difference. But you won't, not ever, be the same again. This is neither good nor bad, it just is. And anyway, too much suffering is caused by trying to hold on to things. There goes your youth, there goes your lover, there goes your health, your wealth, your beauty. All of them useful when they were around, but there are other tools with which to cherish yourself now.

Six: The first thing you give up is a means of comforting yourself with thoughts of suicide. You never know how much you want to live until you're told you might not.

Seven: The second thing you give up is pride. As you do the world will come rushing forward. It is hard to ask for help. But if you don't, you will never understand how much you matter. Or know that the only person who didn't love you enough is huddled inside your skin.

Eight: Your skin is the biggest gift you were ever given.

When the doctors first said I might die, soon, what surprised me was that I didn't wish I'd written more poems. Or even told people I love them—if I love you, you know.

What I wished is that I'd seen more of the world. Let its salt stick to me. I've spent so much time living in my head and in my heart that I forgot to live in my body. Maybe that's why she's in trouble now.

I've been obsessed with achieving immortality through poetry, but when I was told in no uncertain terms that this rickety container has an actual expiration date I knew right then that immortality is merely myth. So, I left that hospital with a horse's dose of right-bleeding-now. We don't get to take anything with us, and anything we leave behind is not one foot still in life. Because once we are dust, we are literally for the wind.

So, on my agenda, with whatever time I have left, is joy.

Because, nine: Anticipatory grief is absurd. When I die I won't be here to miss anything, and engaging in pre-missing seems like an indulgence. It's not that there isn't pleasure in weeping. Why else would we do it so much? But I've got oceans to float. I've got lava to peep. I've got a balcony in the South of France upon which to slow dance with a lover whom I adore down to the spaces between her eyelashes.

Poems will happen, because they are how I process life, but I will no longer mistake them for living.

If I had any advice to give my formerly non-sick self, or maybe you, it would be this: Eat the avocados. Love yourself down to the marrow and out past the rind. Make stalwart enemies out of good people who will hate you with their whole hearts, make it mutual and unconditional— this way you will never be alone with love.

I don't want to be finite, but the fact that we are is what makes even the terror exquisite. So, step out from behind your walls, let the world come forward. Rise to meet it. Turn your precious attention towards God's most tangible gift—this physical world. And while you've got the chance let your beloved skin salt in the wind.

Haima
(Origin of the word "hemorrhage," blood.)

I drop to the curb like a childhood leaving a body.
—Lidia Yuknavitch

Why

Yesterday I saw a house on fire,
thirty-foot flames engulfing
structure. Smoke could not escape
fast enough—first dark, then
white as billowing gas
itself became flammable. Sirens
everywhere, but no water.
People came from blocks
around to stick our noses
into spectacle. Why
fire chose that building will
be pinned down to: cigarette,
electrical malfunction, human
error or malfeasance.
No one will blame the house.
But once our curiosity is answered,
we can put it to rest.

Inside the why of illness
is something that does not rest,
a flicker that turns and turns. Yes,
a tick bit me, as bugs typically bite
me before anyone else
at the campsite. But there is
also the why of that tick,
infected, finding me.

The answer is never punishment.
The answer is never lesson.

"Everything happens
for a reason" is a contribution
made by people who have never
burned to the ground, had others
walk around amid the charred
teeth of their remains.

Why, is a stick with which
I try not to stir coals,
much less leave in sight
of flames.

Fear

is a drop of whiskey hanging on a low branch
                              begging me to put my tongue
                                                          out.

Lawfully

At the pay hospital, I'm met with pressed
lips, can smell the mint white referral
paper before I'm ever ghosted with it.

At the free hospital, nurses lean over my bed,
whisper, "How did you get here?"
They don't mean did I take a bus.

At the pay hospital, it's as if I've turned
into something ticking. Concern
is a town above which doctors
toss my body back and forth.

At the free hospital, I am a Faberge egg,
something to pedestal, protect—
white
as a believable victim.

Privilege: on the street outside
       both hospitals no one sees
       my skin as something to let
       lawfully bleed.

One Live Finger

A few years ago, about everything I do, I started
asking: Is this an act of love or an act of war?

Now that my mortality has found me, this question
has taken on meaning manifold.

When Death puts her white hand to your chest, you know
it is an act of love. That she who gave you everything, can

also drain it away,
                    slowly,

                    or in an instant.
This is how she teaches what is precious. Open

the dolls inside the dolls, find the raspberry there. Find
your mother. Find an eyelash from everyone you've ever

loved. We shed these without regret, without
remorse. The preciousness of an eyelash

from someone who has died is something
of which only the grieving

can begin to speak, can bear to know, never wanted to
know, but were nonetheless taught when Death

put her palm up to the chest of their beloved
and loved them more. Death loves

us more than our beloveds; we must
love her back. If we don't, then we refuse to wed

the one true thing more powerful than ourselves.
Rumi said, "Death is my wedding

with eternity." From this I learn I am destined
for eternal, therefore infinite.

I tell you I love you with my whole heart; this
startles. But I hold none back, no part of my heart

does not love you. I can afford to love like this
because the heart is infinite.

When I say I love, I mean I know
I'm precious, for why else would Death

even bother? Why else would she worry
enough to bring me in

to her kingdom? I might sound crazy, but I've met
Death, been in her arms on yellow gurney

in an observation ward, and let me tell you Death employs
the best singers. They sang for me, said

it was my time to cross over. As they sang
I was unconscious. As they sang I had never been closer

to God. Death is God. All powerful, mostly
unavoidable. I loved the song, but wrestled myself

out of the hands of Death so I could eat one more
mango. With a little lime. Some cherries. Suck on a bay

leaf in an autumn stew. I don't like bay leaves.
Or stew. But now that precious has been pressed

into my chest I know that every single moment might
be my last. So, I pause in front of licorice, wonder

what it has to teach me with its war of flavor,
consider if I can turn it over on my tongue

into love. I think Death has one live
finger, it's how she finds us. Hydrophilic.

Blood-o-philic. Magnet to magnet. Charged body
to charged body. How else would she

find us? Death is not beautiful, while at once
the most beautiful. Elegant. Brutal. Sometimes merciful

or distracted, maybe indecisive. Prone
to change her mind. Her prerogative she exercises

with restraint. But who does she love? The answer: us
all. She is wed to us all—whether or not

we like it we are betrothed to her.
She has no need for battle.

War is her breath,
the smoke in her heart.

       Sex is the fear that made us.
       Love is the war that brings us out.

Yesterday, when they told me I'd be starting chemotherapy,
I screamed.

Today, there are poems piloting out of my fingers.
Mortality has arrived at my doorstep, her arms full

of wedding boughs. Dark bark covered in wet pearls,
all of them fragile, nonetheless perennial. Everlasting

in the way of cycles. When I die, I hope my lover finds
an eyelash on her pillow. I hope she rejoices

with the fervor of a war for all the shedding
that brought me into her mouth.

Product

She tells me my father had a history
of low platelets. Then says, "Volkswagen

is coming out with a new camper.
Maybe I'll buy one, tour the country."

I don't say: "You mean like the one
in which Dad raped me?" Instead,

I say, "Oh,
that would be great, you'd

look great in one of those." Maybe
I got this disorder in the womb,

in the ejaculate moment
his sperm met my mother,

or maybe he injected it into me.
There is no one with whom

I've shared so much blood
product: conception, DNA,

emission inside bleeding me.
Did my father survive this disorder

by being strong, a "Big Buck"
as my mother used to say. If so,

how does a girl survive?
What is the inverse of Big Buck?

The strong inverse, I mean. Because
the myth was that he was strong,

when actually, I was braver. I survived
him; he didn't. I survived

in ways he couldn't: upside down,
in reverse. While talking to my mother, suddenly,

I remember the accident. Our camper hit
a deer, went up on two wheels, haunches high,

whinnied, then slammed down
smashing us onto our side, scrape

of metal as we raked the highway
in reverse. I was the only one not hurt.

Close to the Veil

On a blistering Mother's Day
I feel "close to the veil." Outside
my window a statue appears.
In the trees. Just over
the other side of my neighbor's roof.
My girlfriend is snoozing
at my hip. Dog, quiet across
the room. The statue, purple,
hand in the air, eyes white
as death, gestures to me.
She's a little like the Mona Lisa,
but purple, and animated.
We have a discussion. Not so
much a discussion as an eyeing, fingering
through eye, walking 'round without
walking 'round each other. I fear her, but
she is delicate. Her green scepter
contradicts her eggplant features.

Suddenly, my dog begins to growl. Rushes
from the opposite side of the room to bark
out the window. Distraction!
Look over here! Suddenly,
I understand that animal
friends are not just trained to recognize
intruders, but interlopers, too. Visions,
sneaking suspicions that we're being
sized up as recruits for the dead
army. My bones have never felt
so white. So ancient Rome.

I've heard that Chihuahuas were bred
to draw illness out of a person
while sitting on her lap. My other one died
last year. A tumor on her spleen
that split her open in the night
was the first time
I heard the words, "Bleeding incident."

Instantly, the statue is gone. Just a green
branch. No maroon. Where did
the maroon go? Maybe
the blood. My dog, she was the color
of the darkest bean. I used to tell people
I loved her so much
I'd give her a kidney.

On Steroids, What It Sounds Like in My Head at Night

Slunt mush.
Power plush.
Cunt fuck.
(Survive, survive,
survive. Click.)
This is how
the music comes
out. Fever-ear-
detox-slush-nut.
Cup-plush.
No one's gonna
give a fuck much.
Where are you

in all that sweat?
My brain won't
shut off—
thi ıks it has
something
to do with this,
tired old whore
on a bicycle
too stoned
to remember where
she left her clutch.

First Thoughts

The first time you think, "I'd let them take my leg
if the rest of me could get well."

The first time you think, "How could anyone
love me? Let alone stay?"

The first time you think, "My mother
is going to outlive me."

The first time you think, "I am
a burden."

The first time you think, "I'd kill someone
to live. Maybe that girl over there."

The first time you think, "I wonder if this
is because I did that bad thing."

The first time you think, "Is that me
getting well?"

The first time you think, "Is that me
getting worse?"

The first time you think, "I wonder if Target
has automated wheel chairs?"

The first time you think, "I wish I had cancer—
I hear some people recover from that."

The first time you think, "I hate my friends;
they can walk so many blocks."

The first time you think, "My doctor has a wife. And a house.
And platelets."

The first time you think, "Who will my dog
live with?"

The first time you think, "I could die
today."

The first time you think, "God
is indifferent."

The first time you think, no, it's more like a feeling,
an itching to get out of your own body, a wish
to shrug it off, keep moving, keep running
up stairs after stairs after stairs.

Lessons

In the early days, before I knew
what new rudder had replaced
the old rudder and to which
new blue planet I belong,
my sick-for-twenty-two-years,
gentle, brilliance-for-which-
she-paid-with-her-agony therapist

says: The first lesson is envy.
The second lesson is rage.

The third lesson is a ship that sails
and then sails again, keeps
sailing, again and again, always
            away: The third lesson is grief.

Leaves Behind

I'm trying to get my [**fah**-*th* er]
out of my body.
I'm trying to get my [**fah**-*th* er]
out of my body.
I'm trying to get my [**fah**-*th* er]
out
of my body. I'm trying to get.

The thing about a mosquito
is not the rupture. But what
it leaves behind.

When I think about how incest may have contributed to my disease, I think about what residue is left in a sheath. After slaying, knife stuffed back into contraption, still dirty. Maybe wiped off on the grass first.

But still, part of the new animal's blood freshening the kiss of its ancestor that hangs from hunter's waist. Leather. We think it is a handy skin. Something to hold water, whiskey, weapon. We forget that it held a hope once.

The orphanage where my father grew up made him sharp as a dentist. If a dentist were the sum of all his tools. Trying to peel an orange, if your fingers are dentist tools, must spill a lot of juice. What is the long term effect of all that little orange girl all over the floor?

They say it is possible to learn to sleep with your eyes open. I learned to sleep with my murder open. Paused on the screen in front of me. My night brain imagining every possible escape: This is what I'll do if he comes from the side. This is what I'll do if he comes from behind. This is what I'll do if he doesn't come at all:

Watch. If I were to name a single phrase to describe myself, it would be: Watch Tower. I turned myself into a watch tower. My eyes slept while my spleen stayed alert. My muscles slept while my bones stayed alert.

A hyper immune disorder is something in which your body's system of defense has taken over, refuses to go off duty. Doesn't remember how to go off duty. Mad with all the watching, it starts to attack itself. First the blood. Then bones. Then organs. People with my disease die of not being able to go off watch.

Sheath. Knife. Hide. Watch. Kick. Watch. Sex.
Sheath. Knife. Hide. Watch. Kick. Watch. Sick.

I'm trying to get my [**fah**-*th* er]
out of my body. I'm trying to
get. My [**fah**-*th* er]-watch
out.

Tell me doctor: Am I the sheath?
The knife? (The animal?)
Or the hunt?

Tortile
(Twisted, coiled.)

There have been two great accidents in my life. One was the trolley, and the other was Diego. Diego was by far the worst.
—**Frida Kahlo**

Whimper in My Mouth

If I were to move away
from this pain, I believe
I would choose to do it
slowly. So as to wriggle
from her tight glove, the one
I've learned to navigate with
(her grip on the wheel).
What I would be without her
would be too much all at once.
There's so much moment
in here, so little now
                              out there.
Body gives us pain
to give us ounce. Pound
is something in which people deal
who are on the outside. The ones
gawking in the window. They
pity us; we envy them. That's
the formula. But I tell you,
on this day my daily bread
tastes like no other rain.
So clean, so clean
with this whimper in my mouth.

THE NINE

They call it dissociation.
I call it THE NINE (children)
who live inside me.
Each of them encased
in amber, frozen in a mosquito-pose
of run or sting. Or manage or seduce or judge
or hide. I could tell you their names, but
they'd be stinging me all month.

When the shock/pain/terror/parent-as-apocalypse is too much
      you
              split
      into parts.

My therapist calls them Parts. I know
a woman who calls them Littles.

Each of my Littles goes to see the Lady Talk-Doctor
to get healed. They don't understand
healed. They understand put the knives in the stove
so she can't find them. They understand wear tight shorts
to bed so he has a hard time yanking them off.

On the chart it says D.I.D.
    I   did
    split.
The word shatter doesn't have enough T's in it.

TTTTTTTTTTTTTTTTTTTTTTTTTTTTTTTTTTTTTTTTTTTTT
TTTTTTTTTTTTTTTTTTTTTTTTTTTTTTTTTTTTTTTTTTTTT
TTTTTTTTTTT.

Even when we can't compose ourselves
in public, we sometimes still need to parallel park.
While sobbing. In front of the un-damaged. Who stop
and stare at the way we gun it towards the bumper
in front and gun it towards the bumper in back, trying
to get a good opening, trying to make enough
space (for usssssssss). I tell THE NINE, "It's okay,
those people's nervous systems
were not built by Trauma."

The Fight Back/the Please You/the Hide/
the Seduce/the Sword Inward/the Better Than/
the Fire Alarm/the Littlest/the Hovercraft
and Me (not our real names)
are glad to meet you.

You oughta see my mailboxes.
You oughta see my baggage
tags. You oughta see the sheet I jam
into the door of my closet
in which to wrap us up tight—it's the only way
to get Fire Alarm to stop howling
and Littlest to stop shaking.
Sometimes, sometimes,
I can get Sword Inward
to stop thrusting.

Lady Talk-Doctor says because some of the T happened
before I was verbal, the intervention needs to be non-
verbal. I heard that cows on their way to slaughter
are calmed by a tight chute. So I invented
the sheet-wrap swaddle.

They call it dissociation. I call it containers
in which I horror-stored. Each of which have to be
opened, reheated, rolled out like a lava carpet
and crawled on.

Get-Me-out-in-front-of-THE-NINE
is the finish line. But so far, their little legs
can outrun me at most gatherings.
Especially when I'm trying to park.

My Favorite Hymn Is Velvet

Via the constant search for soft
in which to wrap my infested
with scraped-up feeling skin,
upon purchasing a long-sleeved
velour shirt to wear
inside out to bed, I come to learn

my favorite hymn is velvet.
Velvet, with her millions of tongues,
grassy pelt. All the roots so close
together we think she's one animal
instead of thousands. What if your job
was to be one thread? To stand
with the crowd and shout, "Touch me,
touch me." Held up by brother
leaning on neighbor, at attention
always. When one shivers, all must
shiver: hive mind. Fish
in a school darting all at once,

velvet. In the pew, I run my fingers
along the seat, down my dress and up
again. Thank you, Mother Mary, for letting
such decadence into the antechamber.
We seat ourselves on velvet
for you. Hymns in our hands taste
like peaches rubbed first against
an eager congregation of cheeks.

Smitten

When spending an hour sitting upright
in a wooden chair is a feat,
it's hard to go on a date.

She will take you downtown
where the waitress will try
to prove she's okay with two women
holding hands above the table.
After, on the boardwalk,
you will want so badly
in your necessarily sensible
shoes to stroll easily as summer
couples in the streetlight—
more than you'll want to feel good
in the morning, but

not more than anything. More
than anything, you'll want the test
to come back negative
or even positive, just something
with borders. You'll want the magic word
to roll off the tongue of the hospital
onto your dinner plate: remission.
Because cure is something you put to bed,
pacifier in her mouth,
months ago. A hard baby
to coax to sleep, the itch

for a cure. So, go on the date,
but try not to look
her in the eye in a way
that would cause you to irreparably
fall. Because no one with a choice
should ever have to
do this. Couch-sitting and video-
watching are not a main dish, but
dessert, what happens
after you've been sated

with substance. When she asks
if she can see you again
and again, that way she has of asking
by leaning her shoulder near your head
in anticipation of its droop, pull
back. If she's already interpreting
your droop, it could mean
a variety of things about her
compassion, generosity or
smitten-ness. But smitten doesn't
build kitchens you can cook in. Smitten
barely buys tokens

for the boardwalk, and the real problem
is not what her anticipation
of your droop means
about her, but what it proves
about you.

Second Time

The first time is filled with flowers, showers
of well-wishes, and hands on your back.

The second time is as unexceptional as getting
pulled over for speeding. It's happening

to you, everyone gawks, pities, maybe a few
judge, but no one pulls over to ask if either you

or the enforcer need a glass of water.
Chemotherapy: enforcement. Obedience

to law required. Show up. Hand yourself over. Try
not to cry on the curtains. Ask for a window,

but feel guilty that not every patient
gets one. Last week I didn't vomit and that, that

is a universe. Thank you, God, for the Universe
of Science. All her handy officers, administering

to me with fine gloves. I wish there were a name
for this feeling of trapped, stranded

and alone as if alone were the coldest steel
bar I ever put my tongue on and then tried to run.

Bravery is an old bra into which I sling,
throw a shirt over, then leave the house. Later,

wafting up from fresh cotton, I'll be able to smell
gunpowder wincing out from under my armpits.

Fear is every startle, if I could wear them all
at once, that I've ever owned. Who else,

I wonder, is putting on his loose
garments, piloting himself towards

the hospital, where he will push floor eight
in the elevator? Will I step in front

this time? Gunning for a window? I did
last week. Only half a step ahead, but still

I could have slowed, been polite.
I'm sorry, guy with a face

mask. I'm sorry, guy who's been a patient
long enough to have slip-on shoes.

I hope they cure your leukemia. I hope
we all get exonerated. If bravery is a bra,

then remission is the gown
I'd like to wear down the aisle.

Stages of Chronic Illness

Oh Fuck
>(Lasts a few hours.)

Gratitude for Life
>No vanilla pudding
>will ever taste as vanilla
>or pudding as the little cup
>you're given in the hospital.
>You will weep into your plastic
>spoon with gratitude
>for taste buds, marvel
>that someone was kind enough
>to invent pudding.

Stay of Execution
>When you're released from antiseptic
>clutches and sent home,
>there will not be enough vanilla
>beans to fill your bed, to roll
>around in, while asking,
>"Doesn't this vanilla latte taste delicious,
>I mean, not just delicious, but
>like God himself stirred
>it with his own personal finger?" Your friends
>will love being around you
>in the drinking God's piss phase, because
>you will be so full of life
>it's contagious. Not that they want
>to catch what you have.

Work
>Every day drudgery of the pain,
>unpredictability of the pain,
>fear of the pain, cold fish fact
>of the pain. The pain. You will give up
>uncomfortable shoes, belts, futons
>(too hard), dining chairs (too hard),
>extra curricular activities (too hard).

Science
>	This drug makes me smell like fresh fall
>	leaves. This drug makes me smell like the inside
>	of an alcohol bottle. This drug makes me smell
>	like burning tires. Everything I am
>	smells like sick candy! (But don't click the links,
>	they'll make you want to kill yourself.)

What Is the Point
>	when all I ever do is watch Netflix
>	while waiting for my next doctor,
>	translation: no one who can ever
>	solve anything appointment?
>	During this phase, do not catalog
>	your losses. They're like jeans
>	you've outgrown. Trying to put them on
>	annoys the jeans and makes you want
>	to kill yourself.

No, Really, Why Do I Stay?
>	My therapist says this phase
>	is a boomerang. You'll always find
>	a reason (turns out, you only need one).

What Did I Do to Deserve This?
>	This phase never ends, just takes
>	commercial breaks. Try to stay tuned
>	to your regularly scheduled programming.

God
>	will come in the penultimate
>	hour. The hammer
>	will pause above your own
>	personal clock. No way to know
>	how far he wound it, that guy,
>	on your behalf. But on the day
>	you were born, let's hope
>	he wasn't sore or bored.

Bargaining

       Grief sails daily from the dock—
       there goes another thing
       I can't do/have/be/hope for.
       I'm told the best thing
       is to surrender. But too often,
       I stretch my body beyond
       capacity between dock and ship
       until denial snaps,
       plunges me into fishy water.

Integration

       Grieving and living sit
       at opposite ends
       of a teeter totter, smiling
       at each other, daring
       the other to hop off.

All the Time in the World

You can watch the spider travel
ceiling, or you can spend time
with your friend. Watch the flimsy
way her hair sways, like it's underwater,
has all the time in the world
to frame her beautiful, with or without
hair, face. You can watch the spider
or you can listen to her tale
of how she got taken in by a scallywag,
by something she should have swept outside
along with dust. The spider is making good
time. Your friend is stuck
in heartbreak. Tell her, "I'm not ignoring
you, I'm just watching a spider." Knowing
this will alarm, try not to
alarm. Tell her the drug
they drip into your arm
has a forty percent chance to save, not
that it also has a post-administration year
to kill you. Watch her say, "Ooh,"
the pretty shape her mouth makes, her mouth
makes for the scallywag no more. The spider
will reach the wall, pause briefly
in the corner, before disappearing

altogether. The drug has four syllables
and eight legs. Your friend has high
cheekbones and a laugh that can open
any dam with just the weight of her joy.

Thorax to Match the Summer

I root for the spider
with bees, gnats, mosquitoes,
flies, various unidentified flying
meals, watch him grow fat,
his thorax swell to match
the summer. Until the day a lady
bug waddles slowly outside
my pane. Her antennae peels
air in front of her

for danger. Ever see a spider,
from a corner, thrust toward motion
in his web caused by catching
dinner? You would think
that spider could fly, like his meals.

Maybe, that's the difference
between hope and fear:
hope waddles, while
fear just lies in wait.

Backwash

In 2009, the US National Library of Medicine published the first study among a growing number of research efforts to find childhood traumatic stress "increased the likelihood of hospitalization with a diagnosed autoimmune disease decades into adulthood." The number of hospitalizations increased with a rise in score on the Adverse Childhood Experience (ACE) scale, especially for women.

My score on the ACE is 100%.

I.

On the third day of chemotherapy, I think, "I don't know
if I'm strong enough

to do this. Then I think, "Wait, I've been through
some mess."

But this. This. This

is either an entirely new pool, or one I haven't swum in
for a long time.

II.

My little girl body is shivery and sweaty
on the toilet as I try to push out a teaspoon

of pee, only ten minutes since last attempt.
My body, still unwrinkled, still skin stretching

over forming bone, over what I hated
the world had made me:

girl, girl, girl.

The thing about an infected bladder is not just
having to pee. It's having to pee as if someone

has turned your vagina into an eye
and your urine into mace.

(Now, I pray that when a child has repeated
bladder infections, someone's finger is already halfway

to dialing someone who can help.) Frequently,
I write about incest, but rarely about the actual

physical pain. Emotional anguish,
yes. Dam-destroying, familial natural disaster,

yes. Mutation of watercourse,
certainly. But never about the ripping.

Some of that I repressed. But I do remember bladder
infections. Burning pain and open wound

in the most nerve-infested place, chronically.
Also, what I call: "the yank." Apart. Every year

in the office of Dr. Alan Saunders,
where friction was causing the sides of my vagina

to fuse. I write "yank" and my head
swims. Someone throws herself backwards inside

my skull and goes numb. I don't want to have to fish
that person out of the water, out of the salt stench

where I've been hiding
her for years. I don't want to have to pull

out her carcass and remember
what it feels like to be her

in order to heal. I don't know what it feels like
to be her, because I never fully was. But I also can't forget

what it feels like to be her, because
she has always been me.

We are each other's backwash.
If our body were an ancient cave, these are the things

etched onto our walls, these are our Gods:
sear, tear, scar; blood, piss, cum.

Luckily, cum is not acidic.
But urine is. My enemy,

more than him was my own urine. Which is why
I held it. Which is how it got infected, how

I ended up shivering, cold,
sweaty over the toilet begging my mother

for relief. One of the only times she was nurturing
was when I got sick. She made up a bed

on the couch, let me have TV, Jell-O, juice.
Sometimes, she'd feel my forehead

for a fever with her cheek. Her cheek!
Which I both avoided and loved.

Avoided: neither one of us wanted
to get that close. Avoided: her mouth sometimes smelled

like pepper. Avoided: I knew she didn't want to
touch me, which made me disgusting

to myself. Sometimes she left her perfume on my cheek
as reminder of her repulsion. Loved:

I wasn't going to get yelled at for at least a few
hours. These are some of the things I don't want

to have to dig out of my flesh in order to heal. These are
sensations I don't even want to recall

with my mind, let alone re-experience.
My sick friend suggests I ask the sensations, "When

is the first time I remember feeling this?" as opportunity
to heal, offered by illness. I've done this

with emotions, but never body.
I've been too busy trying to deny

being physical or real. Too busy trying to numb
or control the awakening of my nerve

endings. Now that I'm sick, I find I feel
everything. A hair on my upper lip

catching the wind. My inner ear contracting.
Right now, one thumb is hugging

my opposite hand, as if to reassure her.
I have a scar on my left knee where my mother

told me don't pick that scab, don't
pick that scab. A scar

on my ear from chicken pox. Scars
on my abdomen from surgeries, where I've had

to have bits of him removed from my ovaries, uterus,
intestines, endometrial walls. I have scars

in my most personal places, and an eye
in my vagina that is still stinging. Still trying to blink

poison out. Maybe it's time to ask her what she sees.
But, I can barely imagine pulling her like a dead

herring out of the stink rot water
of my skull. If this is what's required, I avoid myself,

avoid the body until it seizes me, then palliate
and keep moving. How I got so sick

(all systems of my body are now involved
in this disease) is almost beyond me—where it was meant

to be. But now, I must pull matters out of the beyond
into my now. Towards me, pull pain forward,

ask it questions. Maybe I need to lean
back, like all the kind therapists

have done with me, look my body
in her distorted face, and offer compassion.

My sick friend says, "Thank the pain. Thank your body
for managing so much for you

for so long." That she's worn out, my body,
is not her fault. But I want her to keep taking it,

so I don't have to. I suspect what's going to help
solve this is not cognitive, not thinking, but

some kind of doing. Or worse, being.
I imagine that and white hot terror flashes in my diaphragm,

then disappears—like the very possibility of feeling
loss is being obscured

from me. Successfully, by a part of myself
who does her job well. Stealthily. A part

who does not want to be
discovered, but desperately needs to be

discovered. Because despite her heroic efforts
to protect, she's now killing

me. I've been prescribed twenty minutes of meditation
per day, but put it off until tomorrow—

in the beyond. Maybe the body and mind can heal
each other from there, and never have to bother me.

Then I'd never have to take my vagina off the ice,
or heart out

of its block. If a heart is quartered with a jigsaw,
but its pieces are held in place, then frozen

in a block of water, it can appear as if it's still
complete. Not that thing in your chest smithereen-ed

by the woman with the reluctant touch
when she crawled into bed with your father.

Bladder infections involve panties
frequently taken down—something

I tried very hard to not do
in that house. I don't want to have to take

my panties down to ask this body questions.
A woman in a movie goes to prison for life

rather than reveal she can't read. Will I be able
to pull these matters out of hiding

before I prematurely sentence myself
to an early grave? I better go

meditate. No, wait, first—
I have to pee.

Chimera
(A hybrid of two organisms.)

It's a beauty one isn't born with, but must fight to construct at great sacrifice.
—Leslie Feinberg

What Do You Have?

I understand the well-meaning
and impulse to have definition. I want
classification, too, so I know
what bug's exoskeleton to stomp
with the ball of my toe through thick-soled
sandal on hot sidewalk. But,
at the same time,
there's something starting to chafe
about, "What do you have?"

For today, mortality may be closer
on my heels, but no matter how many
borders we etch into the bank,
they will still erode. As will we.
Erosion is law. Water a stone
long enough and eventually it cracks. Wide
open, for everyone to see. But rather
than look for a way to call ourselves
not the rock, might I suggest
another possibility: we take a moment
to ask the granite what sun feels like
now that she is never going to be

the same. Because the answer to that
is much more interesting than the name
of my diseases. The answer to that,
one may be able to apply to the terrain
under sandals that sooner or later
she wakes to find have slipped
onto her feet.

Face of Death

If I could remove the risk, I'd take your hand, lead you to touch the face
of your own death. There are so many things there. Today, I don't have
a choice but to read the face of my death with unsure fingertips. Cold,

wet, sometimes angry, but always tentative fingertips. What is found
there will surprise you, will enrich. Will enrage and delight
and release you. Imagine, this world will not be ours one day. Sooner

than we want it to not be. What will you miss the most? Look beyond
people. Look into the body. What body things will you miss? Look
beyond sex, deeper. Into the mist on your face in a saltwater town.

To the mango on the hottest July day licked from a knife. Into
the green. I will miss the green. This world is so green, green. All
the trees. Lining hospital sidewalks. Parks near hospitals are merciful.

Parks near hospitals are temples of God. Parks, you don't expect to find
on the face of death. Death's face is not cold, but teeming. With life.
All the roaches and all the champagne and all the mirrors casting light

onto walls. We are not in charge. Death teaches us this. With it we are
released into a childlike state of play. Touching death makes us children
again. Not in the humble sense, but in the not-humble sense. The holy

yes, let's touch the stove and jump in the pond and eat scum and wear
a hat of spoons and fruit. Or, wow, I better write that aria. Maybe
I ought to see France. Those things are there, but look deeper. Past

the body. Can you get there? I can only get there in glimpses. Even
with my hand directly on her face. But I urge you to see who made
this mango salad. Who made this mirror slaw. This green, green

gargantuan world. I am as made by what made the world
as the world is made of me. Which is to say everything is
fine. It's gonna be alright. Even if I die. Even if.

Winter

What does winter dream about?
Her fresh shawl on the coldest day
in January. Crisp. Sure. Winter
dreams of certainty. She must
believe in in the afterlife, but how
does winter pray? On her knees
at the sink with her lover locked
out? And for what does winter
plead with God? Winter,

like everyone
prays for a cure, prays for cure
with her methamphetamine
breath. Her exhale white as death.

Is a Fleeting

Sometimes a butterfly lands on you. Butterflies are optimists.
Even given their short lives, they decide to spend their time

in the air. And looking for other butterflies. Cross your
fingers and hope you get mistaken as branch.

The purpose of chemotherapy, of course, is to save
your life by killing

disease. Only the disease and your body have mistaken
each other for themselves. So, aim a fire hose of chemicals

up your nose, ass, down your plea-soaked throat. Then
wait. Butterflies migrate at risk of great

peril. Sometimes having to breed several generations
between destinations. They don't recognize international

borders. US and Mexico, to them, are the same
strip of land they need to wing over. Wing

over wing, over wing, over
offspring until they reach resting grounds. You

could call it an act of mercy that butterflies fly
north at all. Want to adorn our skies

with themselves. After the "therapy" there are tests.
These involve math. And people who get paid

way more and sometimes less than you. Some with jewels
in their noses and some with PhDs. These tests

involve an additional border
crossing. Prepare your country to receive

entry. Prepare your country to put forth
its best goods. Prepare your country to redeem itself

from the last time it shamed the nation, brought down
chemical warfare. Sometimes, a butterfly lands

on you. Alights, rests, flaps
the flags on her back. Remission

is a fleeting. Lucky you have to be
to receive her, be deemed resting grounds. Hold

up your arm. Let them put in the needle. Wait
to be landed on by a merciful something, calls

herself an optimist, who would like
to consider you home.

Yellowing

You can repeat, "This won't break me!
This won't break me! This won't break me!"
without any guarantee
that this won't break you. Drop a tumbler
on a patio, in front of guests, pray,
and it still may shatter, spray
ice across cement, lime
onto everyone's shins. The design

not yours. The timeline,
nope. The maneuvering through raindrops
otherwise known as treatment options—none
of it may matter. Whee! This ride

is pre-programmed without
your consent. Without diagnosis,
you may find yourself
envious of people with chronic diseases,
or rather what is one step away
from fear of death. Or even envious
of for-sure diagnoses. Until the moment
when you're sitting among your peers
in the oncology ward, in a chair
on the ambulatory procedures
floor with a tidy, bruise-y needle
in your forearm, sipping
nurse-served cranberry. The moment
when they wheel in a woman on a gurney
who is green. Not pale, not
yellow, but green. Sort of a gray-green. This
must be what someone looks like
when her death is imminent. From
the way she questions the doctors, you can tell
she's been on this circuit long enough
to know treachery and is hell-
bent on preventing any more
of it. "How many of these
procedures have you done?" she asks.
The resident, taken aback, answers
vaguely. You hear something about a catheter
near her heart. Suddenly, your dress

is so orange. Your life so wide
open with possibility. Even
if you only have a couple of months left
in the hourglass. This day's particular sentence
is only for as long as the drip takes
until you, shakily, and with effort, yes,
but upright walk out of here
into the yellowing, yellowing sun.

Burden of Reassurance

My girlfriend has just returned
from the beach. Where she's spent the afternoon
with friends. "They asked about you," she says.
"What did you tell them?" I ask.
She answers: "Chemo."
I nod.

She says, "But then I told them about your new
doctor. People want good news."

Ah, they do. In addition
to hosting the flames, spectators
would like the house to supply

sunglasses. Briefly, I consider intentionally
not getting well. Just to stick it
to them—obviously, absurd.
But still, let's check our Hollywood endings
at the edge of the roof, onto which,
before it's all gone to ash,
you might dare crawl with me,
where we might sit awhile, look up, marvel
in silence at the breadth of the wide,
wide Universe, of which we are both lucky,
at the same time, to be a part.

Corpse

And then I realize what I'm trying to wiggle
with my tongue out of my teeth is actually
me. Where the roof of my mouth is coming

off in slats. A corpse comes alive
with maggots. Post mortem animation.
Lookit us wave our hands, hands, hands.

Large Flakes

And the past came down
in large flakes, irregular snow, much
of it coughed from my throat, the throat
of the past where pink was
my esophagus, and I remembered

how to laugh. Last year said,
"You better buy new shoes."
This year said, "Don't bother
to waterproof." Next year
says, "Hey stupid, look over here,
come swim in what has melted,
call it vacation and try not to cry
or open your eyes under water."

Some things are still burning,
one of them is my reflection.

Mothlights

On the hearths of free care hospitals
are pink-slipped casualties
begging under mothlights.

He Did Not Come

I had a dog once, no, correction, I loved
a dog once to whom I attached as if she were
a person, no, correction, as if she were
a bone in my arm. She healed me in places
I didn't know I was broken,
taught me three things: I am
not toxic to living things, capable
of commitment, and lovable.

When she died, I grieved like my child
had died. I don't aim to minimize
anyone's parenthood, but to illuminate
my own stunted growth. So damaged,
I could only stand to bond to an animal
who had no human fist
or tongue to use against me. When she died,
I went more than a wishbone insane, came
home from the scene with cherry blossoms
on my shoes, tore all the clocks
off the walls, and wept like
there had been a massacre in my
heart. Her name

was Lily. I had a husband once, no,
correction, I loved a man to whom
I attached, and thanks to Lily, could let
love me. He was the first and last human
fist into which I curled and called home.
Six weeks after Lily died, he
left. I went whole-bird insane. For months
I couldn't read time right, the sun looked
sick, cherries tasted of sawdust. For years,
I couldn't bear to smell anyone else's
breath. I did not think I'd live.
The grief, I told everyone who would listen,
was like having a slow bleeder, but not being
able to reach the hole with my finger
to stanch the flow. There was a trickle, gently
depleting my will to live.

When I got sick: I wanted him, wanted
to smell her. A whiff
of either one of them
used to tell the animal inside me I was safe.
He did not come
home. She could not come home.
So, I just kept punching the clock, clocking
in to my shift, here on planet blossom.
Automatically. Because inertia dictates
what direction the minute hand goes.

My disease is often triggered
by some other event, typically another illness
but sometimes trauma. My disease
means my blood has gone mad
with inertia. There's no mechanism to plug
the tiny, naturally occurring splits
in my vessels.

Having no prior experience
with attachment, I didn't know how
to stop the course of devotion,
how to call myself someone
else's mother, make myself someone
else's wife. Sometimes when I dream
of dying, I see her on the other side
of a river. My nose anticipates
what it will be to approach the warmth

of her ear. When I dream of him, I
wake up with his smell all over my hands,
with the smell of my slow, self-eating
suicide all over my hands. He has a baby

now. Someone else he takes to the doctor.
I'm told his wife is a nurse, good
at patching things up.

How to Strike at the Heart of a Girl

Be a girl. Be a friend. Goad
her secrets into your palm.
Memorize her vulnerabilities
like you would memorize how
to make a lover cum. Soothe
and soothe her. Make her think
she has soothed and soothed you.
This way, when the truck comes
for her trust they will bring
a bigger truck, back its garbage
mouth through her fluttering
street. Masturbate to the beeps
like they are a victory bell. Apply
lipstick, drive across town
to where that boy is waiting
with a stake for her chest. Her
chest—that swath of target
on which you can't wait to lie
down and fuck. Because,
you think he could never betray
you like he's betrayed her.
At least, not until your other friend
walks by. Prettier. Younger. Hunter
who's memorized your secrets.

When it happens I want
you to know I tried
to warn you. Showed you
the welts, never thought
you'd use them like a recipe
for how to get me
to murder myself.

You are better than this. We
are better than this. If me
tangled in every moment
with him is what's making you
hot, then maybe you oughta
put your tongue in my
mouth. Fish around for a key
to the place where I can un-imagine

this. Where I can not lose two
of my hearts at once. For
the record, the one I had for you
was always bigger, made
for the moon to envy. Her gravity,
legendary. I think if girls kept
our loyalties to each other
there would be no hell.

Tell me the world is not shaped
like a bomb. Tell me the bed
in which your knees part
is not our daughters' demise,
our daughters' daughters' demise,
our daughters' daughters' daughters
demise. The way men get us
to act against each other makes
the world of women a machine
with self-destroying parts.

I am not a boy. I am a girl. We
both know what that means:
that we were built to face
this moment. This impossible
pushing of each other
into opposite lifeboats.
I will miss you like I would
miss my health. I will
miss you like I would miss
every green flutter
on every single street. I hope
he treats you like
he treated me. Not
because you deserve it. You
don't. But better to meet
immediately master's sword
than his blanket. Blanket
is but a lure to get you
to curl up, go to sleep
while he hunts. For heads,
for fools, for girls like us.

Resist. Come home. I pray
for you to say you choose
us both. Not some joker
on a horse about which they lied
to both of us. You are the horse. You
are the rider. You are the land
and the tower and the streaming
hair up which to climb to rescue
yourself. Dignity is not sacrificed
for happiness. Trust is not
something to be wiped up
with a napkin. A friend is a
kingdom, a kingdom, a kingdom.

Lilac Tree

For seventeen years I've had
a friend who is a lilac tree. I call
her Miss Lady. She lives in a secret
park near my house. In the spring
I kiss her leaves and cheer
for her blooms. In the winter I pet her
and promise spring. A few years ago, half
of her body went gray, stopped sprouting,
blooming. Since I've been so ill
I look to her for mentorship
on how to lose part of me
and still have the courage to push
life out of other parts. This very year,
her gray half started sprouting again.
I petted her, kissed her leaves, asked,
"Miss Lady, do you think I can, too?
Do you think I can do this?" Her answer
was flutter. And extra blooms.

That Syllable

1986
I cut off the frosted pink fingernails I have worn since the seventh grade. None of the lesbians look like me.

1987
The first time I tell a woman I'm attracted to her, I say, "There is something I need to tell you or I'm going to vomit." She is a boyish and I am a girlish, although neither one of us will ever mention this. Because, here, we have shamed gender out of queerness and believe androgyny will deliver us.

1988
I'm standing to the left of the jade plant in Connie and Cheryl's house when I first hear the syllable that makes the rugby players draped all over the furniture sneer. I laugh, too, but as I run my fingers over the stubble of my imposter haircut, I memorize that syllable, Femme, with the wide-open mandible of my heart.

1989
Chicago, who has lured me away from my dirt road and small town, finds the AIDS epidemic suddenly upon us. Lesbians serve and serve, add our bodies to ACT UP. But some of us, tired of being talked over and told to be patient, leave to create Queer Nation and the Lesbian Cancer Project, because what is killing us are too many things.

1990
Following a speech I give at a Queer Nation protest, the androdyke who will go on to direct the pinnacle lesbian film *Go Fish* says, "Wow, I didn't think you had that in you. I mean, you wear all those pastels." I go home to polish the buckle on my Femme closet.

1995
In Seattle's Red & Black books, one of the nation's last cooperative bookstores, I find copies of *The Lesbian S/M Safety Manual* and *Stone Butch Blues*. They bring a heat to my core and flush to my cheeks, but I read them in the car after work, in secret, because my androgynous girlfriend has banned them from the house.

1997
For the first time, I go out in public as myself. Seattle's Re-Bar is hosting a drag king show. I wear full body fishnets, a leopard print bra and a black

miniskirt trimmed in fake fur. At home, after, I wash the shame of side glances and double takes off with my make-up, but feel the teensiest bit of relief that I've let my secret out.

1999
The panel at Toys in Babeland tells us they no longer want to be called lesbians, and broadens a possibility: Transgender. The community erupts into battle lines. Chosen families suddenly act a lot like those of our origins.

2001
He tells me I'm pretty and all the blue birds hidden under my skirt suddenly take flight. Soon, the butches start painting me as straight. I wrestle them: lose and win and lose, until we lose all track of the meaning of queer kin.

2002
We fly to Reno, because, there, you don't need a birth certificate. I lean my open neckline far over the counter as the clerk distractedly stamps our coveted license. We're hitched and in our hotel room in half an hour.

2003
We try to ruin each other with nonmonogamy. And fail.

2006
We try to ruin each other with nonmonogamy. And fail.

2007
He wants a baby. I try and try and try, but cannot bring myself to bring an unwanted child into the world with me as her mother.

2008
He tries and tries and tries, but cannot stop coming into his new destiny as father.

2010
He is remarried fifty-nine days after the ink is dry. I come apart in ribbons. The baby is born in October as the leaves fall. I start saying to anyone who will listen that grief is like having a slow leak, deep inside, that I can't reach to plug with my finger.

2011

My body begins to sprout a crop of red freckles. At the hospital they say sometimes, for "no reason," platelets fly from their posts like gulls from a sinking ship. My blood will not clot. Bruises bloom where I bump myself—I'm told to drive slow and watch my head.

2012

He does not call; I bleed. He does not call; I bleed. The doctors ask me for my spleen. I say no, go home to talk with God, who through Rumi, says, "Death is my wedding with eternity."

2013

Everyone is going to picnics. Everyone is going to Pride. Everyone is starting to be everyone again. The T has begun to be less of a tag on to LGB. I don't call to congratulate him on the second child, or join the June parade. Instead, I stay home and bleed.

2013

Chemotherapy is a lily. I am to crawl inside her and try to pollinate. There is no other hand I want to hold when they puncture my vein, but he is changing diapers and beaming at his new wife. So, a gay brother steps forward, agrees to let his eyes be the ones I look upon when they turn on the drip. Family is a name that will come right up out of the ground and surprise you from an underground spring.

2013

Am I still a Femme if I shit the bed on my first night of chemotherapy while sleeping next to my new butch girlfriend? Am I still a Femme if all I can wear are sweatpants and no mascara? Without the heels and feathers and sequins, what, in her heart, makes a Femme a Femme? Is it next to whom she sleeps?

2014

I sleep alone.

2015

I sleep alone.

2016

What makes a Femme a Femme is not her clothes. Is not her hair or shoes. It may not even be her desire. It might be her history. It might be her song. Because Queer community is a remedy, my bleeding starts to slow. Inside me where platelets come once more to roost, I know that Femme is not defined by the outside circumstance of my skin and who does or does not press against my freckles. What makes a Femme a Femme is not for whom she bleeds. What makes a Femme a Femme is the person for whom she repairs her leaks. Which is to say, herself. Death may be my wedding with eternity, but Femme is my wedding with myself.

Gignoskein
(To know.)

We must shift from a politic of desirability and beauty to a politic of ugly and magnificence.
—Mia Mingus

Doctors

We listen to doctors. Because doctors
have science. And we have desperation. Science
is the religion of the desperate.

Science is the last resort for people running
to catch up with our illnesses, for those
pounding on the door of the bus after

its door has closed. It's why the third thing
I did when I got sick was apply
to medical school. The second was kiss

the sidewalk outside my house
on the way home from the hospital.
The first was too private

to tell, but involved whispering.
The doctors pump us full
of their after lunch sleepy nap thoughts,

because lunch was good and we're just another
what-do-I-have-what-do-I-have? As if
the answer is a prize in a raffle.

What you have, ma'am, is something—
we're not sure, but here's a Latin
name which roughly means

        we have no idea why your life has run ahead to catch the bus

while you're back here trying get your coat zipped.
I once fell for someone because on our first date,
as I struggled with a zipper, he dropped

to his knees and zipped my coat for me. I'm an easy
mark when feeling helpless. So on Tuesday
I throw back and swallow something

else with three syllables and a hard round body.
Whose promise is to rocket this mystery
out of my system, whose correct

pronunciation I'll learn from someone with
the good sense to invest
in science before, without warning,

the sole light in the library of his body burned
out. The bulb is out, my mother would say, then
head to the pantry. Some things

have a pantry: the kidney, for example,
has a back-up. So do lungs. The liver
has lobes. The spleen is much like a welcome

mat, handy if you have one, but not
essential. However, without a roof,
you're screwed. The roof of my health

blew off. No one can tell me why,
for sure. Some doctors say, we think
you're making it up. Pouring all that weather

over your own furniture. We go
with doctors, follow ones with the kindest
smiles, or biggest pencils, or harshest

attitudes (they must be smarter).
I'd follow one of them into a canyon
lined with coal while holding a decanter

of gasoline in one hand, match in the other,
if I thought he could read the hieroglyphs
in my blood. Instead, I am here, too sick

to procure my own headlamp. Too tired
to object, protestation itself being useless
at this juncture. What would I say, to whom

would I say it? Excuse me, my bulb
seems to have burned out, can you check
your pantry? Instead, on Tuesday,

I take another gamble
on something that could make me
sicker, weaken me more. But

it's been prescribed
by a priest of science,
and hell, it's all I got.

Diagnosis

Death is my wedding with eternity. —Rumi

And the diagnosis comes

down.
                    Like a light snow.   Or a palette
of newspapers.

READ. ALL. ABOUT IT!

The diagnosis comes
down. It has a name.
The name is: Back-
lash. The name is: Anti-
Christ. The name is:
You've just run out

of roll over minutes. The name is: Welcome
to the method of your death

we just don't know when
yet. The diagnosis comes

down. It sounds like rain in February in Seattle. Repetitive.
It has a name, its name is: Redundant. Just because it has a name

doesn't mean it was making me any less
sick before I knew its motherfucking name.

It has a name. The name is motherfucker. If motherfucker
meant genocide—I should not use

that word. Still, its real name is not enough
for all the things it is extinct-ing in me. The diagnosis
comes down in partial crowns.
To be worn sideways.

Like royalty who are asleep,
or drunk. Or passively malevolent.

It has a name.

Its name is: Someday
you, too, will wear
this crown of human

frailty. Then everyone will look
at you like you're the sad homecoming

queen at the reunion. Twice divorced, or widowed
by things that have names:

Cancer.
Car accident.
Heart attack.
If you want

to recognize something call it by its name. Call
it and it will come, roll over, bark. The diagnosis

comes down. I want to feel relief, but I feel
my anticipated relief dragged into the bushes

and beaten. (Whether or not you know his name
makes it no more or less rape.) The diagnosis is stuck

in my teeth.
The diagnosis
is stuck
in my throat.
The diagnosis
is written
in my chart in someone else's
handwriting. Next to my weight,

which I always tell them I don't want
to know, because once I had another diagnosis: Vanity

(anorexia) and it almost killed me. Sometimes
I wonder at what a privilege it was to have vanity. Before

this thing had me turn over my good veins to the nurses
on the oncology ward. I remember the lady who

put her wig on the handle of her wheelchair, said, "Larry,
I'm putting my wig right here, don't let me forget it." Her

diagnosis came
down. Its name
had a fistful
of hair in its mouth.
The diagnosis

comes down. I think, how did I get someone else's
diagnosis? No, that's not how you pronounce my name.

    My name is grace.
    My name is verb.

My name lilacs in early June. Deep
purple. Early thaw. Something

to hang your hope on. My name is not sad
sack of ballooning skin. My name is not blue

circles under my eyes. My name is not "Here,
shit in this plastic hat then bring a spoonful to the hospital."

My name is not "This could kill you any minute
have you tied up your affairs lately?" My name

is not I.V. immunoglobulin or forty thousand
dollars worth of charity chemotherapy.

    My name is Tara.
    It is not Disease.

And just because I have it doesn't mean anyone gets
to define me by it. Or distance themselves

from it, meaning
                me. The diagnosis came down.

Verdict.
Conclusion: Incurable,

but nonetheless now something that lives
inside me. Let us take her out to dinner. Let us

welcome her to the family.
Let us rip

lettuce with our hands and serve it next to the bread
we'll obviously be breaking

with our new guest. Welcome, Disease.
Welcome home to my body that I had previously only shared

with a handful of lovers. Welcome to this roof
over our heads. You're here for as long as I

am, an arranged marriage, so let's
make the best of it. Cheers. You've come

down.   This is my side
of the bed,   but you're welcome

to make me rethink what might be
        closer to the bathroom.

        There you are again: I have to pee.
        There you are again: I have to wheeze,
        I have to crawl

out of this bed of pillows and relieve one pain before
sliding back into another. Why did you bring

your set of aches? What are you planning
to paint on the walls? Do I get to keep

my feet? Do I get to keep
my heart? Let me keep

my heart. This, I ask, Disease,
if we are going to share a home, then let me keep

this four-chapeled room with which I'll navigate the world
for both of us.

There will be a before and an after,
                            a BC and AD

of diagnosis. Her name
will be as holy as your own.

It has to be. Otherwise,
                    there is not enough room in this house.

Dear Diagnosis, I swear, when I learned
your name, I heard
                    wedding bells.

Cure

The illness is rough. But the things they do
           to save you. That is the real
invasion. You will think you are occupied
when they deliver the diagnosis. But you ain't
           even met an army until they try

                                        to cure you.

First, they turn you into a bug
light. Light you up for days. Drive
              the life-force right along with the disease-
                     force into the zap. Crueler than that,
              they eventually unplug you, leave
you in the hot sand. Make you
                        walk back   to civilization.

Only now your hands
are mitts. Your feet an absurd concept
when your legs don't work. You should
be prepared for sore elbows. Burned
elbows.   Carry lotion. Carry water.
                        Carry nuts. Carry barf receptacles.
                        Carry your shame in your teeth. Spit

and spit and spit   it out. Doesn't matter
if it's in front of people. They will (or won't)
                  forgive you. Understanding (or not)

           is a privilege
           of the rich, the healthy
I mean. No matter what anyone thinks,
the crawl is the same. Towards the pink
light. Towards the new worm
wriggling just out of reach.
That is who you want to be.

Is It Just Me?

Treatment, Day 7:

> I have an urge to stick a butter knife
> in my ex-husband's grandmother's thigh
> (or an electrical socket). Worthy
>
> note: I've never been angry with my ex-
> grandmother-in-law for any reason. (Except
> when she botched her grandson's pronouns,
> but that was over a decade ago and it's probably
> time to let sleeping fish lie.)

Treatment, Day 3:

> I'm so nauseous it feels like an entire school
> of live sardines has taken up residence
> in my stomach in which they're fucking
> each other—while standing up!—and partying
> like it's 19-motherfucking-pass-the-tequila-99!

Treatment, Day 4:

> Fish belly will prompt me to take
> what the doctors call an "anti-nausea pill,"
> but what I call the entire Wizard of Oz
> come to life in my skull. Now in Technicolor!
> With shoes! There's no place like home,
> there's no place like…uh, is it possible
> the anti-nausea drug is actually making me
> nauseous? Or rather, so high, meaning taller
> than all the trees in the Emerald Forest,
> that I'm experiencing vertigo?

Treatment, Day 6:

> I am totally certain it's time
> to call my new lover to say, "I don't care
> if you hang out with your slutty ex-girlfriend,
> it doesn't bother me at all! Just send me
> a memo!" then burst into tears. Because
> nothing says, "Ooh, pick me, pick me!"
> like a little homicidal possessiveness.

Dear Impulse Control,
thanks for showing up
at the party without
our pants. We look so, um,
what's that word? Oh, right—
mentally deranged in this outfit.

Treatment, Day 8:

Dear Doctor Sardine,
While you are, in fact,
at least according to several websites,
a Lyme Disease treatment genius, I'm wondering
if you might put me on a lower dose? Oh,
this is the lower dose? We're just waiting
until I equalize to increase? Great,
I can't wait to see what kind of Surrender-
Dorothy, Tequila-Shootin' Grandmother
Slayer I turn into next time.

P.S. Does anyone smell smoke,
dog feet, or 1986 Polo cologne,
or is it just me?

Grief Body

It's as if the grief has made its own body
inside my body. Which would be fine
if it would sit still, but the constant
turning, the trying to relieve itself
of bed sores. I feel her turning
in me, this unwanted fetus grown
toddler, howling, "No!" Chronic
malcontent, always wanting
bottle, nipple, but nothing

pacifies. I keep trying to lose
her on the trail. Leave her on someone
else's doorstep, but by morning
the authorities have found me,
returned what is rightfully
mine. I want to smother her
in her sleep; I want to push
her over the falls. There are not
too many countries in which
this would not be considered

child abuse. It's as if the grief
has made her own body, inside
my body. Feral and learnedly helpless
at the same time. Keeps her own
hours, yowls at all

hours. When a mother leaves
her child, she also leaves a body
inside her child's body. Maybe the body
is sleeping until the child is forty-something
when her husband leaves. Regardless,
something is bound to wake this child
who is hungry, starved for decades,
inconsolable. Now the daughter
has a ravenous wolf on her
hands. It's as if the grief has
a body of its own inside
my body. What will console her
is as easy as befriending wolves.

When I Say Grief

I mean yesterday I had to sit on the bathroom floor
for twenty minutes because I noticed the doorknob

to our, to my, bathroom had scratches from our wedding
rings. Two days ago the song to which we walked down the aisle

came on the radio. I turned ice cold and thanked God I wasn't driving
over a bridge. These days I do everything I can to avoid them.

Last week I woke mid heart-hiccup from a dream out of which
I could still smell him on my hands. They don't tell you how this

will alter your body. Rip out the seams and re-sew you into a new
garment. Maybe one without arm holes. This helplessness

must be what it feels like to have fins and gills on dry land.
When I say grief I mean there are whole months like having fins

and gills on dry land without the relief of dying. Yesterday, muscle
memory typed his name at the top of an email to someone else

because their names share the first three letters. But now, there
is another woman who memorizes his earlobes. On our first

date, in the time it took a drop of rain to fall from his lobe
to shoulder I formed a whole new definition of permanent.

Of what it means to meet a seam that keeps re-sewing itself;
no matter how many times you rip

the stitches the needle will find you in the dark. When I say grief
I mean I'm that weird girl at parties trying to look anything other

than how I actually feel and not answer "Apocalypse" when I'm asked,
"How are you?" How can it be possible to cry for a year?

I want to shout at anyone who will listen, "I've been crying
for a year! Do you see me?" Grief makes you feel invisible.

Because if anyone could see the you you're becoming they'd surely
give you something. But there is no something to give.

On some days you'll stick around if only because you're curious
what could possibly be on the other side. Before he left

I asked him what anyone else who tries to love me should know,
he said, "That your heart is infinite." Goddammit what I wouldn't

do for a different mathematical diagnosis. Mother, I can't
seem to find my hands inside the garment of my skin. It's cold

in here. When I say grief I mean no mother's milk. If there
were a scalpel for such things, I could want but still not

be able to ask for an amputation. Because despite it all, this
experiment called loss is freakishly interesting. Littered

with the exquisite torture of weeping. Strangled with the story
of dry land. When the first fish walked, do you think he wanted

to leave his family behind? Having discovered that some things
are impossible to suppress? I don't know who I'll be on the other

side, and the fucked thing is he probably does. And he probably
doesn't. When I say divorce, I mean walking away from the only

reliable map of yourself. Stepping into a place without footprints
like you are the first person to ever have feet. Disorienting

is an understatement when you know where your home is sleeping,
seventy-two miles away, but you will never breathe his night-

air again. None of us remember the trauma of our birth, but some
of us carry its thumbprints on our skulls. When I say grief

I know what's required is to reach in and pull out myself. But I can't
find my hands. So, I'm just gonna have to settle, no,

I'm just gonna have to God-walk
out of here on these terrible but magnificent feet.

Wishes She Still Were

The first lesson is envy. —My therapist

Everyone keeps saying, "I'm so glad you're well."
I'm not

well. Sometimes I say
I've gotten back so much. My sicker friend
disagrees, says, "Yeah but
you're still not yourself." The day she does
my trunk splits. Wood,
when split, reveals

whorls in the crevice of its demise,
some of them look like curves
of women, some of them look
like scarves. Others refuse
to be classified, don't swirl
at all. Inside the oldest trees there are dead
middles, upright hollow
cylinders. When split open
their trunks look like surprised
or horrified throats.

She means well, when she confronts
my denial, hopes I'll take
better care, not push
so hard. Maybe she's right, but
in the coming weeks
without my denial
I'll be more aware
of the grain of the pain,
the timber-splitting sound
of my life cracked in half.
In the coming months I'll think
about the handle of an axe: she
has her own story. Her own
memory of the forest,
of straining towards light,
only to end up threaded into
a blade. Forever doomed to chop
away at who she
wishes she still were.

Mows Around

The second lesson is rage. —My therapist

Normally I'm a person who mows around
dandelions, wants to protect
their spindly reaches
for sun. But after a week of treatment
that sets my whole upper body
on fire. Not as in fever,
but as in do you remember, as a child,
scraping your leg against cement?
An abrasion about the size
of a dollar? The way the blood beaded
and your mother sprayed Bactine?
The wheeze, hiss
of the bottle? Do you remember how,
on that second day, your heartbeat
struck the wound, woke you
with its throb and pulse,
ache that was hot, too sensitive
to touch?

Normally, I'm a person
who mows around dandelions,
talks to them, tells their butterscotch faces
they're doing a good job. But
after a week of treatment that makes
it feel like my ankles, arms,
and eyelids are covered in second day
abrasions, when I encounter a group
of young women at a counter
in a sandwich shop, listen to all six
equivocate, then order extra avocado
and chardonnay, while I pray
to be able to remain upright, I

imagine the satisfaction
of stabbing a sardine-sized blade
into one of their skulls. The way the wealth
of her un-punctured health
would buckle under my authority.

My hand flies to my throat, I think
I'm not just
in physical pain—suddenly
aware that the epicenter
of the second day abrasion
is under my skin, below
my chest plate, the crying-out
whimper of my heart.

Upon Watching Someone You Love Lose Their Mind

You can forgive the lost tickets. And the moon gone rotten
under the seat of the car. You can forgive the contradictions,

paradoxes shaped like razor mazes. You can forgive
the yelling spittle on your collarbone. And the fear. Even

terror. You can forgive the way the boat takes on water
when you suggest a trip to the doctor. You can forgive

the way the couch you're sitting on jumps
when it's kicked. You've already forgiven being left

in the parking lot without a coat, in February, in a city
in which you know no one's phone number. What

you can't forgive, or maybe can't get over
is the suspicion. The after you've boiled and served

your tongue, being told you're not giving enough. Or
you're giving too much—you are soft in all the wrong

places, leaking fluid, not truly naked when you're bald-assed
in the backyard hammering a window into your

conscience. What you can't forgive is the suspicion.
The investigation upon the half of a half hour

or more. My friends call it paranoid, but I have a hard time
putting such an ugly sticker on the locker

of someone I love so much.
So, I call it confused.

I wish you would ring my door, eager
on my stoop with a fistful of lilies. Apologies to scent

my room. Where I would lead you by the tie and not break
eye contact. There, we would peel off our cottons

and mistaken identities. The sight of my freckles
would make you remember that I am that safe landscape

you fantasized about for years. You were never wrong
about me. Until you were so wrong

about me. I know they came for you. And I did not come
in time. I have to live with that. But I want it to matter

that I came at all. I keep hoping that if you can just think
hard enough about who I am, you won't want to call me

those names, the ones your rapists left in your mouth.
But it doesn't work like that. Sometimes, someone safe

enough to get close, getting close, rings all the old fire bells.
You will be right when you say it's not reducible

to this, because there are ways that I'm soft. But
there are not ways I'm dangerous. Not anymore. Not since

I shaved the taste of my own rapist out of my mouth.
I wish we didn't have to lose our minds so completely

in order to heal. I wish the world didn't see
the crazy on us, or if they did, labeled it nothing

more than a sane response to having one's wick lit. But I know
we all do have to go into the stinking rotten cave

of echoes in order to rescue the parts of ourselves
that got left behind. I just wish you didn't have to go in there

alone. I want you to know I tried to go with you. Until
the cost was too high, and the too-high was not when I thought

you might kill me in the kitchen. The cost was too high
when my mind started getting colonized by what invades

you, when I believed what you said
about me. When I started losing logic, because

I was always arguing with your suspicion.
Who knows, you might be right. I might be just

not enough. Or too much. I only wish that our two tender
selves got to sleep next to each other tonight.

The last time I talked to you, hope leaking
silently down my face, I was still a suspect.

I still miss you as much
as I would miss my own name.

"After"math

and the waves roll
in as tall
as crooked
magicians,
and the fires
roll in as hot
as pouring steel,
the walls close
tighter than a
nuthouse jacket,
the doors shrink
and I'm caught
in your duplex,
the windows lock
and I'm caught
in your car,
you're driving
and accusing me,
again. Sometimes,

just before dawn, I collapse
and dream that I'm pinned to table,
a biology specimen, while you stab
little white flags into all my

sins. Eighteen months and I still wake up yelling. Yelling. Yell.Ing.

       The world has stopped
  fitting.
      Has found itself no longer
a shoe. More like a rolling pin
      that someone has strapped to my feet and
           then yelled, "Run!"

Do you remember when you screamed
into my collarbone that I caused your disease
(which is scientifically impossible)? You may have caused
mine. We both know this. I forgave you
instantly.

I
      still
do.

When it rains I think how good that you're not
in Seattle. I know a low ceiling makes you panic.

Panic is not an excuse for everything.

Does the world need you as its hero more
than I need to tell?

Maybe.

Is my voice a small price
to pay for what the prophet brings?

These are the terms of my truce:
There is no truce, because there's never
been a war. There
was only you, raising rifle
and white flag at the same time.

What the Doe Feels

What must the doe feel
with that target on her
lover's skull? What much
of her body must she want
to throw in front
of bullet? A prize, she must think.
He is, yes, a prize. But leave him
be. Leave him to wild up
the forest as nature designed.
Don't make me a widow.
Don't make my future a window
from which our children
will never be able to wipe

the grief. When you say
you're going to wear a tie
on the plane, my torso blushes
with heat. With a built-in lean
towards masculinity. Straight
women understand this lean-towards,
this nature-installed flush for the ways
of swagger. But what they may not
have had to develop so keenly
is my nose for gunpowder.
The way fear lives right next

door to my desire. I know you
can handle yourself on the plane,
in any public restroom
you have to visit between there
and here. But also, there are days
I want to stitch myself
to your hip, or send me in to play
a round in your stead. To find
the rifle first, meet it with my nose.
Plead with hunter with my breast, "Take
me, take me." Leave my buck alone
to her own unstoppable nature.

Things Sick People Know That (Sometimes) Healthy People Do Not

I.

The body is not just
about beauty. In the tub,
although skin that channels water
is sallow, still nothing is so precious
as what houses all one will
ever be. In other words, how old people
still find each other desirable
is they don't reduce
their lust to vanity.

II.

Misshapen is just another front door
                              to holy.

III.

There is pain contained within your house
that is much worse than what you think you already know
about suffering. This capacity, you'll be shocked
to possess. That your will to live is still a factor past
this education will disarm you—in that it will fire
holes in any window you had into burden. Or bravery.

I know a woman whose health has been boarded up
for twenty-six years. She is my hero. I used to think
that bravery was standing up to a bully, or no-rope
mountain climbing. Now, I think it's your teeth
falling out in your hand and still finding reason
to grin.

IV.

When a chronically ill person appears
at your event, I want you to know:
a) You're an Ace. Your party is worth
consequence, b) Please find that person
a comfortable chair, a front row seat,

and tell the MC to not drag
things out, because what it costs some
is not reducible to door charge.

V.

Rage is the lung of illness.

VI.

Envy is the bed.

VII.

There are people to whom you will describe your symptoms
well past when it's socially appropriate. You will know
it's well past appropriate and still not be able to stop
yourself. It's called: desperation doesn't factory-install
boundaries and embarrassment is least of my worries. Because
sometimes all you need to fall asleep after you've been robbed
is to tell someone, "I've been robbed."

VIII.

It hurts all over. In the soul. In the God-place.
Spleen and rib. Blood and hearth. The chest
of a chronically ill person is full
of old Valentines. Don't be surprised
to find her counting them, repeating,
"I was lovable once, I was something
to prize."

IX.

The only thing guaranteed is the now. Even if
the now is full of ants. Full of hopes
it's hard to know whether to bring a crumb
of cake or stomp. Because hope, to the sick,
is not always something you want
following you indoors.

X.

This list is not as sunny as the role model I'd like
it to be, not something to roll up and store
in your attic for when you need it later. But it is a root
to which we are all attached. Deep,
thick and nonnegotiable as vulnerability.

XI.

There are not just ten things the sick know
that the chronically healthy do not. There is a nation
of tales passed down by other patriots. When I found
myself sick and panicked, the only worthy
advice I ever got was to chant to myself, "Other
people have felt this, other people have felt this."

XII.

The Land of the Sick is not my chosen residence. Like family,
it was assigned. Like family, I'm at least glad
if I have to go through this, I'm not
the only one.

XIII.

The last thing sick people know
that the healthy (sometimes)
do not, is that the bathtub
is a place to leave lights on, survey
damage, toast the treasure,
and with still so much left to lose,
sing.

Dares Ask

A spider can live for years,
over-winters in a hole in a board,
a bit of leaf debris.

I've started having cognitive symptoms.

At dusk, the moon rises
up over the Cascades, bold,
early. The spider comes
out of her corner to gawk
with me at the near-daytime pearl.

An inability to tell a story
all the way through.

I want to ask the spider how she makes it
through the cold, turns her blood to ally,
antifreeze.

This afternoon, I told my girlfriend
I wanted "snorkel tacos" for lunch,
unable to locate the word salmon.

Were I smaller,
she would bind me up tight,
puncture my skull with her teeth
as I've seen her do with several good bees.

Funny how often I lose
my concentration, how often
I snorkel through an afternoon.

A fat bee, already dim from the chill
of October, plunges into the spider's net.

People shout on Facebook,
"Isn't it lovely how the weather
is cooperating?" I think, "With what,
your legs?"

I wonder, how many days left
for the spider to hunt? How
will she choose her shelter?

The beautiful thing about speaking
different languages is that neither
the spider, nor I, dares ask
how long the other will last.

Hemostasis
(To arrest a flow of blood.)

Write the story that you were always afraid to tell. I swear to you that there is magic in it, and if you show yourself naked for me, I'll be naked for you. It will be our covenant.
—Dorothy Allison

Dark Yellow

You could say it was a dream.
Or vision.
Or not real.
But what's real,
and what isn't,
is just a bone
for philosophers
to pick over.
Regardless of their
verdict, this is how
it went down.

All day I'd been
feeling close
to the veil.
Post-treatment
chemotherapy sickness
and new symptoms
lurking in the foreground
waiting for me
to float into them.
Abruptly, I felt
a hoof on my chest,
that I recognized
as buffalo.

Hours later, after
I was unhooked
from machines,
tubes & wires,
after the nitroglycerine
had faded, I fell
unconscious,
felt myself begin
to lift up
out of my bones.
Behind it
there was singing,
a warm, brightening Light—
the curtain, it was
dark yellow.

Advice to Daughters with Cruel Mothers

1. Get a dog. The consistent and hungry gaze of "I forgive you" cannot be underestimated. A well-timed "I forgive you" can rewire your shame habit.
2. Don elaborate outfits of which your mother would disapprove. Wear them in public with friends. When you get home at night, look in the mirror and approve of yourself.
3. Eat. Deprivation is the religion of girls who were raised by cruel mothers. Resist. Every meal is a revolution you can win.
4. Break up with critical female mentors. You are not more worthy if you can endure their unkindness. You are recreating history.
5. Do a yearly sweep of mean people. If you feel bad about yourself after seeing a friend, slip out of that friendship like a hand outgrowing a glove. Seek friends in whose eyes you are birthday cake.
6. When the birthdays come around, try not to think about the body you came out of—it will make you susceptible to picking up the phone. Do not pick up the phone on your birthday to call anyone but the dog rescue.
7. Grant yourself the right to not answer her calls. For a week, a year, five years. Do what it takes to keep your heart above water. Do not feel guilty about it.
8. Weave your guilt into curtains (they're sure to keep the light out). In the morning, you can throw guilt open to greet the light, who has always had a more realistic vision of who you are than your mother ever will.
9. Keep what is steady near you. When you blow it up and blow it up and blow it up and blow it up and blow it up and blow it up, rebuild. Eventually a foundation will stay poured. Never doubt that of the steady beneath you, your feet are worthy.
10. People who bring excitement and words like "soulmate" into your life are too often poison-laden candy. They taste great, but leave you with holes in your integrity and strangely inexplicable whiplash.
11. Do not mistake dissociation for disinterest. Disinterest can be just another attempt to preempt rejection, which by the way won't kill you. That it feels like it will is a memory. Because the core wound of anyone betrayed by her mother is my least favorite word— abandonment.
12. It's okay to be shattered.
13. It's okay to be shattered into pieces you keep tripping over. Just pick them up and add them to the bouquet.

14. It's okay that you're never going be "normal." It's okay if "okay" is a concept you won't grow into. Some people's "okay" is different— an inner tube with no air in it, in which we just walk around in the shallow end and make it look like we're afloat.

15. It's okay when you lose things. Those mittens may never come home, but your panic is a flashback—to being punished for being fallible.

16. You may have distorted, probably paranoid thoughts. This is not shameful. This is adaptation from having had to be on constant watch.

17. You may have distorted magical thinking. This is not shameful. This is adaptation from having no reality-based source of hope.

18. You may have distorted thoughts of inferiority and superiority. This is not shameful. This is the result of having had your image shrunken or distended depending on what met your captor's needs.

19. No matter what your mother says, your memory is not a liar.

20. Trust your body. She remembers everything.

21. Map your self-sabotage. Name it after your mother. Envision her as a child; treat the part of you that sabotages yourself the way she should have been treated. Love your inner saboteur with a ferocity that could reset the axis of motherhood.

22. When your dog dies, get another dog. Unlike mother, you don't get just one. (And dogs are a great way to re-parent yourself.)

23. Get sober. From everything that makes you feel hungover. Shopping. Romance. Vodka. Driving the exit ramp with your eyes closed. Married men. Broken lovers. No matter how long it takes or how many times you have to try—seek recovery.

24. Replace your addictions with things that burgeon into backyard gardens that feed you: art, activism, and the biggest antidote to anyone who ever sought to diminish you—faith.

25. Don't date daddy. Period.

26. No matter how tough you think you are, you are not impenetrable. There is no such thing as so damaged that you can't be further damaged.

27. You are not too sensitive. No matter how many times you wail because someone stole your parking spot, what other people call "overreaction" is just the result of a nervous system that was BUILT BY TRAUMA, MOTHERFUCKERS!

28. The world isn't built to respond well to those of us with diverse nervous systems, so seek help. Find a woman whose job it is to sit in a chair and love you. Pay her to show you you're lovable. Let her give you a diagnosis that basically means, "Somebody fucked with me, therefore I have license to be fucked up." Eventually, you will trust this woman to help you pin the tail on reality. It's okay—five to ten years is a really short time to trust someone like that.

29. No really, you're going to need a therapist, because ultimately it's not okay to act out our trauma on other people.
30. When people tell you that therapy is not a basic need, say, "Hmm. I guess no one tried to murder your soul when you were a child." And then offer them the opportunity to be reincarnated as your mother's next daughter.
31. With the thousands of slivers, just under your skin, that refuse to come to the surface and out—those things she said about you. I don't know what to do with those. Mine ache regularly. Some seep. Perhaps we could get tattoos to connect the dots. I wonder what the result would look like—perhaps a chandelier upon which to hang crystals. Crystals all over our bodies, dangling from our mothers' insults, reflecting the light and swinging erratically when the past roars by.
32. There will be a last call for a good life. Get on it. Ride that train through the mountain of resentment to the other side. Do not doubt that there is another side. And you deserve it. The reason to get beyond resentment is not her—it's you.
33. It's harder to get rid of resentment than dandelions in a dandelion factory. When you find they've regrown, it's best to relocate. Sometimes there is a geographical cure, meaning distance between you and your mother.
34. In order to thrive it's necessary to befriend the demons inside you. They're just little kids who made up strategies and then got stuck. Especially love the worst one of you. She too holds wisdom. She too holds a scream that was just too much.
35. You will not want to do this, but it's most important. Befriend, no, adopt the littlest you. No matter how many times you've left her by the side of the road, that's just what you were taught. I promise she's not trying to kill you. And she's not rotten. She's perfect—the Universe chose to put breath in her chest for a reason.

You may feel allergic to this little one. But perhaps some day, because it happened to me, after decades of trying to starve that girl out of me, eventually, through a lot of work with my lady in a chair who I pay to love me, I came to not begrudge that I need that little girl as much as she needs me. I tried to kill her, repeatedly. But you and me and all the daughters of cruel mothers, which even includes our mothers, we deserve to let our original little selves live. Because when it comes to the way out—she is the flashlight.

Woman Artist

A woman artist is someone who has come to terms
with her own solitude. Out here on the big water,
she may encounter other lonely souls. But always
finds herself retreating, back, through arched tunnel
into the quiet and rowdy cove of her mind. She

will find God there. And earwax. And laundry.
And summer. And rot. The file cabinet in which
she keeps these has a will of its own. Drawers
roll open in the middle of the night to reveal
just hatched cuckoos, needy as the very drive

that told her to pass on the pantyhose. A woman
artist's best ally is another woman artist. Someone
with whom she can be vulnerable enough to ask,
"Was it right, did I do the right thing when I left
him, aborted her, gave up on keeping safe

as my mother." Another woman artist will know
not to answer, for these questions are the Creator
herself. Whose impulse resides in fissure.
In other words, regret is fuel—is fear,
and to be trusted. A woman artist trusts fear,

for fear is more faithful than the dog
next to whom she sleeps at night. The dog
named Doubt. To whom her enemies have been feeding
scraps under the table since before she was
born. A woman artist's enemies are best kept close

as dinnertime, if only so she may predict
from where the next sear will come. Quickly she learns
her forging is in the scalding. Her strength bred
from bad reviews and laughter. Let the crows come,
she will say one day, without terror. For crows

are a raucous river against the night sky
and something that agitates is exactly what I meant
to paint today. Exactly what I meant to shape
out of red clay and antonyms. So, go ahead,
get agitated at what I wrote. Agitation is what I cash

to pay for potatoes. Were I to have children,
I would dress them in agitation and send them out
to agitate for bringing back agitation in school.
But I don't. So, instead, I will merely remind us,
with my presence, that it's possible to be female

and not afraid of solitude. Or an empty nest.
My nest is not empty, it's filled with a promise
I made to myself as soon as I cleared the kitchen
counter, that although I will always respect women
whose primary purpose is to tend the brood,

I just wasn't meant to be one of them. Rather,
I was meant to serve by answering the call
of an impulse so loud that I turned down anything
anyone ever said was safe in order to heed it. I
let the Juris Doctorate and the husband

and the financial promise of my aptitude roll by.
I gave up my own genealogical line to spend
more time with the loneliness in which I can best hear
God. If you are a girl who finds herself feeling odd
on career days and at birthday parties, look

down, you may have been granted a very rare
pair of slippers. That you can use to pace the path
between your head and chest, head and chest
until something remarkable flares out. Something
so potent we try to scare girls away

from its edges. But what Virginia Woolf taught me
is that not only does an artist have the right to her source,
which is, of course, her solitude. But lurking just inside
that cove is the birthright of every woman: the hallowed
and most singular state of her exquisite originality.

Wine Cloth

There are days that the fabric of my personhood turns porous
in my hands. Sometimes, I hardly believe I survived,

navigated that much violence while so small, a violet
in the midst of a grape-stomp. Perhaps ironically,

it wasn't the rapes, wasn't the beatings. Well, maybe
a little, it was the beatings, but more the outright

contempt. The being hated and disgusted by my own
mother. Her face, pressed close to mine uttering

words a child should never know
let alone have to digest. What do they do

with the grape skin? Trash it, I'm sure. But what about people
who might live to see another day if they're allowed

to consume the leftovers. Humans are resourceful. I bet
somewhere, tucked into some shameful shelf is a recipe

for grape-skin pie. And a person who's alive because
her great-great-grandmother taught it to her great-

grandmother who taught it to her grandmother and so on
down the line. Sometimes the fabric

of my personhood is little more than wine cloth
in my hands. The resilience

of a recipe that requires a sweet crop
be stomped this many times.

My, My, My, My, My

Take that thing that happened. To you.
Open it like a concealed rose. Hold it up
to the nose of someone else. Let them
tell you that you still smell sweet. So

sweet. Let that person who loves you pluck
petals out of the gully of your wound. Let
her shave them into points and sail them
back into your heart like paper airplanes. For

that fist at the center of your pulse
is of what you have always been made, despite
what trauma taught you: to tip your fingers
in thorn. Use them now to shred the sheets. Shred

the night. No one should have to sleep under that much
dark or on that much polite. Slit the sky.
Let the Gods fall out. The ones who could've
let that thing happen in the first place.

God after God after God. Catch them
in your pockets. Catch them in your chest.
Put the God back in your chest. Until
you believe in yourself. Again. Repeat.

Take that rose, the one your flesh wounds
around. Open it and open it and open it.
Toss bits of your scar into the air
like goddamned wedding rice. Or bird seed.

Let some of them sprout. Into so much green,
green new day it makes your shins hurt
with how much you want to run—forward
and greet the world without all those

red whorls, those old scars, those stuck stitches
in your side. And we, we will marvel at your
silhouette. My, we'll say. My, my, my, my, my!
Doesn't she run like an un-flowering?

One Hundred Beautiful Perfect Percent

For Miss Lady

In a secret park near my apartment I have made friends with a lilac tree. Her name is Miss Lady. Nineteen years I have known her name. In April I cheer her blooms. In October I kiss her leaves and promise spring. She is shaped like a very deep V, one that's been filled out with a lot of flutter.

The year I got sick, half of Miss Lady went dormant. Half of her stopped speaking leaf. She was still a V, but the live part of her was a lean. That year I was only able to visit her once. I told her I was sick, but she didn't flinch or stop inviting me to parties, just stood with me, like a good friend, without the need to distance herself.

In the first year of my illness, I almost died five times. Five times I was in the charity hospital while they pumped the part of me that kept going dormant back into my veins. The part of me that kept trying to cut itself off from the trunk, they threaded back into me. I leaned a lot that year. On friends, walls. Over the sides of chairs, trying to keep myself upright.

Miss Lady went through a whole round of seasons four blocks from where I lay wishing that sick were not my new name. Wishing that I were trotting down to the park to flirt with my friend and marvel at her deep green, heart-shaped leaves.

In the second year of my illness I lost a lot of friends. People stick with you for the first blush of imperfect, because they love you and want to see you get well. When you don't bounce back, but instead enter a long thin tunnel of uncertainty, they return to their fully live lives, to things that call full blush to their cheeks and lips.

In the second year, Miss Lady and I had a conversation about how just because she was only half blooms didn't mean her perfume was any less sweet. Or her purple less deep. When I told her, "Miss Lady, you are still worthy, even half dormant," we both knew I was hoping it was true.

In the third year of my illness I experienced ten minutes of normal. On April 20, 2013 at noon, I was able to sit fully upright without forcing myself. I gasped, thought, "I'm getting well." The feeling passed quickly, but I memorized its outline. The next day, I went to see Miss Lady, only to find that out of a small portion of her dead half she was sprouting new blooms. They were tentative, shy and lavender, but full scent and quivering.

I leaned on Miss Lady and cried. She knew I knew she was teaching me how to come back to life, how to regain even part of who I used to be.

As another set of seasons tucked their shoulders and rolled, each into the next, my ten minutes of feel-better became twenty, became an hour, became whole days when I feel almost fifty percent of my old self. If you've only been twenty percent yourself for whole years, fifty feels like full fuchsia.

Here, in my fourth year of illness, I know I'll probably never be fully well again, but I will take whatever the indiscriminate laws of nature mercifully return, and marvel at its vibrancy.

This morning, two years past my first ten normal minutes, I lace up and set out to tell Miss Lady the good news. The day is flawless. Bees buzz in cherry trees. Birds trill instructions to their mates to, "Pick up worms on your way home."

At the mouth of the park, my heart flutters at the prospect of seeing my old friend, getting to kiss her leaves and shove my face in her blooms. I round the corner, dash through the pines and into the clearing—only to find Miss Lady gone. Someone who believes that imperfect is an eyesore has cut Miss Lady down. Someone who believes that fifty percent isn't worth living has stolen my friend.

Shocked, I stumble wetly from the park.

All the way back to my house, full-bushed lilacs boast their scent all over the neighborhood. For the first time in my life I find the smell bitter.

From Miss Lady I've learned that some victories will only ever be partial, but partial is sometimes all you have. Meaning that even if you're only half of what you used to be, you deserve to be let bloom. Because no matter what anyone else believes, you are one hundred beautiful perfect percent alive, until you're gone.

Epilogue

Two dark nights ago I stole into the park, just to kiss Miss Lady's severed trunk. To my surprise, out of the top of her stump, there are shoots. Right here in January, Miss Lady is coming back. Stepping out and preparing for June.

Epilogue II

In early May, Miss Lady's shoots begin to wilt. I study, then cut. Dip her cuttings in root hormone, plant them in perlite, peat moss and prayer. Four weeks and we will know, the two of us, if our friendship ends here.

Back at the park, I water her first body. Days later, she is near crumble. My face leaks onto her leaves. My cheeks salt her trunk. I smooth the sawed off evidence of her former limbs, kiss her dark wounds. Whisper, "It's okay, Miss Lady. You do what you need to do."

Every morning, from the terracotta in which I've nestled her shoots, I show Miss Lady to herself in the mirror. "See, Miss Lady, this is what I would be missing," I say. And then I chant—"Root, root, root."

Flew

Last summer, while the healthy
were out picnicking and dashing
skip-ily across crosswalks, I was making
friends with a spider who had taken
up residence in a corner
outside my window. She was fast
and brutal, would wait for sunset
when the bugs came out, then
pounce. I watched her suck the life
outa the heads of several bees
while I cheered. Until the day a ladybug

clearly out past curfew, started
waddling across the window
towards the web. I considered
tapping on the glass
to warn the lady, but
then I thought, why should just
the pretty survive? Who am I
to re-route fate? So, I did nothing
but watch life dish up life's
terms. Me, sick and brutally
awed in my pink chemotherapy gown
watched as God marched
that lady nine inches, two inches, three
millimeters away from the web,
when to my marvel at the velocity
of life, there in the twilight,
she flew.

Acknowledgements

For above and beyond:
Tamara Lewis. Dr. Marty Ross. My brother, Bill Hardy. My niece, Betina Hardy. Karen Finneyfrock. Sara Brickman. Greg Brisendine. Ebo Barton. Lucy. Lily. Jim Walker. Kathleen Nacozy. Kristina Armenakis. DP Sheppard. Carol Lellis. Amy Cornell. Debbie Carlson. Derrick Brown. Dorothy Allison. Sharon Hardy. Peter Hoelzl.

For all your support:
Cedar Addison Smith. Sini Anderson. Daemond Arrindell. Heather Askeland. Elissa Ball. Michelle Bombadier. Tatyana Brown. Jason Carney. Allison Durazzi. Brian Ellis. Elaina M. Ellis. Shira Erlichman. Amber Flame. Paula Friedrich. Anis Gisele. Ash Goddard. Dr. John Harlan. Tobi Hill-Meyer. Garfield Hillson. Maya Hersh. Dorothy Frances Kent. Miss Lady. Marc Mazique. Brian McGuigan. Rachel McKibbens. Mia Mingus. Mary Anne Moorman. Angel Nafis. Bif Naked. Mindy Nettifee. Zoe Norvell. Madi Parker. Emily Ann Peterson. Susan Rees. Sonya Renee Taylor. Kayla Shelley. Dejuan Skelton. Joe Paul Slaby. Lisa Slater. Jim Stapleton. Fritha Strand. Fred Swanson. Casey Tonnelly. Frances Varian. Martha Wakenshaw. Sophia Wight. Chase Williams. Alex Ziperovich. Lauren Zuniga. The many, many people who contributed to BOOST. And: Harborview Hospital nursing staff. SLAA. Bent. Gay City. Richard Hugo House. Vermont College. Antibiotics. Chimeric proteins. That night on Charley Young Beach on which I touched the moon.

Tara Hardy is the working class, Queer, Femme, chronically ill founder of Bent Writing Institute for LGBTIQ writers in Seattle. She grew up under the great big sky of Michigan, but now writes at the majestic hem of Mount Rainier in Seattle. Her first book of poems *Bring Down the Chandeliers,* published by Write Bloody Press in 2011, primarily addresses being a father-daughter incest survivor. Tara holds an MFA from Vermont College and is a former Richard Hugo House Writer in Residence, former Seattle Poet Populist and alumnae of Hedgebrook. She is an instructor at Seattle Central College, Richard Hugo House and Path With Art. She is also the Arts Director at Gay City. Tara is a daughter of the United Auto Workers and has been engaged with anti-violence and liberation work since she was old enough to sing at union rallies. Tara has also been a maid (uniform included), park ranger (tractor included), convenience store clerk (threatening clientele included), activist (self righteousness included), and teacher (apple not included). To book her for a workshop or performance, you can find her at www.tarahardy.net.

IF YOU LIKE TARA HARDY,
TARA HARDY LIKES...

Ceremony of the Choking Ghost
Karen Finneyfrock

Courage: Daring Poems for Gutsy Girls
Karen Finneyfrock, Mindy Nettifee & Rachel McKibbens, editors

Floating, Brilliant, Gone
Franny Choi

Racing Hummingbirds
Jeanann Verlee

Any Psalm You Want
Khary Jackson

Write Bloody Publishing distributes and promotes great books of fiction, poetry and art every year. We are an independent press dedicated to quality literature and book design, with an office in Los Angeles, CA.

Our employees are authors and artists so we call ourselves a family. Our design team comes from all over America: modern painters, photographers and rock album designers create book covers we're proud to be judged by.

We publish and promote 8-12 tour-savvy authors per year. We are grass-roots, D.I.Y., bootstrap believers. Pull up a good book and join the family. Support independent authors, artists and presses.

Want to know more about Write Bloody books, authors and events?
Join our maling list at

www.writebloody.com

Write Bloody Books

After the Witch Hunt — Megan Falley

Aim for the Head: An Anthology of Zombie Poetry — Rob Sturma, Editor

Amulet — Jason Bayani

Any Psalm You Want — Khary Jackson

Birthday Girl with Possum — Brendan Constantine

The Bones Below — Sierra DeMulder

Born in the Year of the Butterfly Knife — Derrick C. Brown

Bring Down the Chandeliers — Tara Hardy

Ceremony for the Choking Ghost — Karen Finneyfrock

Counting Descent — Clint Smith

Courage: Daring Poems for Gutsy Girls — Karen Finneyfrock, Mindy Nettifee & Rachel McKibbens, Editors

Dear Future Boyfriend — Cristin O'Keefe Aptowicz

Dive: The Life and Fight of Reba Tutt — Hannah Safren

Drunks and Other Poems of Recovery — Jack McCarthy

The Elephant Engine High Dive Revival anthology

Everything Is Everything — Cristin O'Keefe Aptowicz

The Feather Room — Anis Mojgani

Gentleman Practice — Buddy Wakefield

Glitter in the Blood: A Guide to Braver Writing — Mindy Nettifee

Good Grief — Stevie Edwards

The Good Things About America — Derrick Brown & Kevin Staniec, Editors

Hot Teen Slut — Cristin O'Keefe Aptowicz

I Love Science! — Shanny Jean Maney

I Love You Is Back — Derrick C. Brown

The Importance of Being Ernest — Ernest Cline

In Search of Midnight — Mike McGee

The Incredible Sestina Anthology — Daniel Nester, Editor

Junkyard Ghost Revival anthology

Kissing Oscar Wilde — Jade Sylvan

The Last Time as We Are — Taylor Mali

Learn Then Burn — Tim Stafford & Derrick C. Brown, Editors

CPSIA information can be obtained
at www.ICGtesting.com
Printed in the USA
FSOW02n1710131116
27291FS

9 781938 912641